AIR FRYER RECIPES

Publications International, Ltd.

Some of the products listed in this publication may be in limited quantities.

Pictured on the front cover (*top to bottom*): Green Bean Fries (*page 216*) and Spicy Korean Chicken Wings (*page 18*).

Pictured on the back cover (*top to bottom*): Bang-Bang Chicken on Rice (*page 136*) and Mozzarella Sticks (*page 9*).

Microwave Cooking: Microwave ovens vary in wattage. Use the cooking times as guidelines and check for doneness before adding more time.

WARNING: Food preparation, baking and cooking involve inherent dangers: misuse of electric products, sharp electric tools, boiling water, hot stoves, allergic reactions, foodborne illnesses and the like, pose numerous potential risks. Publications International, Ltd. (PIL) assumes no responsibility or liability for any damages you may experience as a result of following recipes, instructions, tips or advice in this publication.

While we hope this publication helps you find new ways to eat delicious foods, you may not always achieve the results desired due to variations in ingredients, cooking temperatures, typos, errors, omissions, or individual cooking abilities.

Let's get social!

 @Publications_International

@PublicationsInternational

www.pilbooks.com

TABLE OF CONTENTS

ENJOY YOUR AIR FRYER

ENJOY YOUR AIR FRYER

Do you love fried foods but try to avoid them? You no longer need to worry.

The air fryer is your answer to preparing fried foods without the extra calories, fat, or mess in the kitchen. You'll get the taste and texture of fried foods—crispy, tasty, and crunchy—that you love and crave, without the added guilt often felt when consuming them. Plus, you'll soon see how your air fryer is so easy to use, cooks food faster, and provides a no-fuss clean up.

You'll love the ability to prepare fried foods in your air fryer, but you'll also soon find that you can prepare all types of other foods, too. Make everything from appetizers to meals to sides and even desserts! Why not try cookies or muffins? What about trying marinated salmon or a tuna melt? You'll even love the taste of roasted vegetables. You can bake in it, grill in it, steam in it, roast in it, and reheat in it.

Choose from more than 100 ideas here, or create your own.

Now get started and have fun eating and serving all those healthier foods without the added guilt.

HELPFUL TIPS:

- Read your air fryer's manufacturer's directions carefully before cooking to make sure you understand the specific features of your air fryer before starting to cook.

- Preheat your air fryer for 2 to 3 minutes before cooking.

- You can cook foods typically cooked in the oven in your air fryer. But because the air fryer is more condensed than a regular oven, it is recommended that recipes cut 25°F to 50°F off the temperature and 20% off the typical cooking times.

- Avoid having foods stick to your air fryer basket by using nonstick cooking spray or cooking on parchment paper or foil. You can also get food to brown and crisp more easily by spraying occasionally with nonstick cooking spray during the cooking process.

- Don't overfill your basket. Each air fryer differs in its basket size. Cook foods in batches as needed.

- Use toothpicks to hold food in place. You may notice that light foods may blow around from the pressure of the fan. Just be sure to secure foods in the basket to prevent this.

- Check foods while cooking by opening the air fryer basket. This will not disturb cooking times. Once you return the basket, the cooking resumes.

- Experiment with cooking times of various foods. Test foods for doneness before consuming—check meats and poultry with a meat thermometer, and use a toothpick to test muffins and cupcakes.

- Use your air fryer to cook frozen foods, too! Frozen French fries, fish sticks, chicken nuggets, individual pizzas—these all work great. Just remember to reduce cooking temperatures and times.

ESTIMATED COOKING TEMPERATURES/TIMES*

FOOD	TEMPERATURE	TIMING
Vegetables (asparagus, broccoli, corn-on-cob, green beans, mushrooms, tomatoes)	390°F	6 to 10 min.
Vegetables (bell peppers, cauliflower, eggplant, onions, potatoes, zucchini)	390°F	10 to 15 min.
Chicken (bone-in)	370°F	20 to 25 min.
Chicken (boneless)	370°F	12 to 15 min.
Beef (ground beef)	370°F	15 to 17 min.
Beef (steaks, roasts)	390°F	10 to 15 min.
Pork	370°F	12 to 15 min.
Fish	390°F	10 to 12 min.
Frozen Foods	390°F	10 to 15 min.

*This is just a guide. All food varies in size, weight, and texture. Be sure to test your food for preferred doneness before consuming it. Also, some foods will need to be shaken or flipped to help distribute ingredients for proper cooking.

Make note of the temperatures and times that work best for you for continued success of your air fryer.

Enjoy and have fun!

APPETIZERS & FINGER FOODS

MOZZARELLA STICKS

MAKES 12 SERVINGS

¼ cup all-purpose flour

2 eggs

1 tablespoon water

1 cup plain dry bread crumbs

2 teaspoons Italian seasoning

½ teaspoon salt

½ teaspoon garlic powder

1 package (12 ounces) string cheese (12 sticks)

1 cup marinara or pizza sauce, heated

1. Place flour in shallow dish. Whisk eggs and water in another shallow dish. Combine bread crumbs, Italian seasoning, salt and garlic powder in third shallow dish.

2. Coat each piece of cheese with flour. Dip in egg mixture, letting excess drip back into dish. Roll in bread crumb mixture to coat. Dip again in egg mixture and roll again in bread crumb mixture. Place on baking sheet. Refrigerate until ready to cook.

3. Preheat air fryer to 370°F. Line basket with parchment paper; spray with nonstick cooking spray.

4. Cook in batches 8 to 10 minutes, shaking halfway through cooking, until golden brown. Serve with marinara sauce.

TOASTED RAVIOLI

MAKES 6 SERVINGS

1 cup all-purpose flour

2 eggs

¼ cup water

1 cup plain dry bread crumbs

1 teaspoon Italian seasoning

¾ teaspoon garlic powder

¼ teaspoon salt

½ cup grated Parmesan cheese

2 tablespoons finely chopped fresh parsley (optional)

1 package (10 ounces) cheese or meat ravioli, thawed if frozen

½ cup pasta sauce, heated

1. Place flour in shallow dish. Whisk eggs and water in another shallow dish. Combine bread crumbs, Italian seasoning, garlic powder and salt in third shallow dish. Combine Parmesan cheese and parsley, if desired, in large bowl.

2. Coat ravioli with flour. Dip in egg mixture, letting excess drip back into dish. Roll in bread crumb mixture to coat. Spray with nonstick cooking spray.

3. Preheat air fryer to 390°F. Poke holes in ravioli with toothpick.

4. Cook in batches 5 to 6 minutes, turning once, until golden brown. Add to bowl with cheese; toss to coat. Serve warm with sauce.

FALAFEL NUGGETS

MAKES 12 SERVINGS

SAUCE

- 2½ cups tomato sauce
- ⅓ cup tomato paste
- 2 tablespoons lemon juice
- 2 teaspoons sugar
- 1 teaspoon onion powder
- ½ teaspoon salt

FALAFEL

- 2 cans (about 15 ounces each) chickpeas, rinsed and drained
- ½ cup all-purpose flour
- ½ cup chopped fresh parsley
- 1 egg
- ¼ cup minced onion
- 3 tablespoons lemon juice
- 2 tablespoons minced garlic
- 2 teaspoons ground cumin
- ½ teaspoon salt
- ½ teaspoon ground red pepper *or* red pepper flakes

1. For sauce, combine tomato sauce, tomato paste, 2 tablespoons lemon juice, sugar, onion powder and ½ teaspoon salt in medium saucepan. Simmer over medium-low heat 20 minutes or until heated through. Cover and keep warm until ready to serve.

2. For falafel, combine chickpeas, flour, parsley, egg, minced onion, 3 tablespoons lemon juice, garlic, cumin, ½ teaspoon salt and ground red pepper in food processor or blender; process until well blended. Shape mixture into 1-inch balls. Spray with nonstick cooking spray.

3. Preheat air fryer to 390°F. Line basket with foil; spray with cooking spray.

4. Cook in batches 12 to 15 minutes, turning halfway through cooking, until browned. Serve with sauce.

BAKED ORANGE BRIE APPETIZER

MAKES 6 SERVINGS

1 **sheet puff pastry (half of 17¼-ounce package), thawed**

⅓ **cup orange marmalade**

2 **tablespoons chopped pecans (optional)**

1 **round (8 ounces) Brie cheese**

1 **egg white, beaten**

1. Roll out puff pastry to 12-inch square. Use knife to cut off 4 corners; set aside scraps.

2. Spread marmalade over center of pastry to 1 inch of edges. Sprinkle pecans over marmalade, if desired. Place Brie in center on top of pecans. Brush exposed dough with egg white.

3. Gather up edges of puff pastry and bring together over center of Brie, covering cheese entirely. Pinch and twist pastry edges together to seal. Use dough scraps to decorate top of Brie. Brush lightly with egg white.

4. Preheat air fryer to 370°F.

5. Cook 8 to 10 minutes or until golden brown. Serve warm.

LAVASH CHIPS WITH ARTICHOKE PESTO

MAKES 8 SERVINGS (ABOUT 1½ CUPS PESTO)

3 pieces lavash bread

¼ cup plus 2 tablespoons olive oil, divided

¾ teaspoon kosher salt, divided

1 can (14 ounces) artichoke hearts, rinsed and drained

½ cup chopped walnuts, toasted*

¼ cup packed fresh basil leaves

1 clove garlic, minced

2 tablespoons lemon juice

¼ cup grated Parmesan cheese

To toast nuts, cook in preheated 325°F parchment paper-lined air fryer 3 to 4 minutes or until golden brown.

1. Preheat air fryer to 370°F. Line basket with parchment paper.

2. Brush both sides of lavash with 2 tablespoons oil. Sprinkle with ¼ teaspoon salt. Cut to fit in air fryer, if necessary. Cook in batches 6 to 8 minutes, shaking occasionally, until lavash is crisp and browned. Cool on wire rack.

3. Place artichoke hearts, walnuts, basil, garlic, lemon juice and remaining ½ teaspoon salt in food processor; pulse about 12 times until coarsely chopped. While food processor is running, slowly stream remaining ¼ cup oil until smooth. Add Parmesan cheese and pulse until blended.

4. Serve lavash with pesto.

NOTE: You can also toast walnuts in preheated 350°F oven 6 to 8 minutes, if preferred.

SPICY KOREAN CHICKEN WINGS

MAKES 6 TO 8 SERVINGS

- 3 tablespoons peanut oil, divided
- 2 tablespoons grated fresh ginger
- ½ cup soy sauce
- ¼ cup cider vinegar
- ¼ cup honey
- ¼ cup chili garlic sauce
- 2 tablespoons orange juice
- 1 tablespoon dark sesame oil
- 18 chicken wings or drummettes
- Sesame seeds (optional)

1. Prepare sauce. Heat 2 tablespoons peanut oil in medium skillet over medium-high heat. Add ginger; cook and stir 1 minute. Add soy sauce, vinegar, honey, chili garlic sauce, orange juice and sesame oil; cook and stir 2 minutes.

2. Rinse wings under cold water; pat dry with paper towels. Remove and discard wing tips. Brush with remaining 1 tablespoon peanut oil.

3. Preheat air fryer to 370°F. Spray basket with nonstick cooking spray.

4. Cook in batches 16 to 18 minutes or until crispy and browned and cooked through. Remove to paper towel-lined plate.

5. Add wings to sauce; toss to coat. Sprinkle with sesame seeds, if desired.

JALAPEÑO POPPERS

MAKES 20 TO 24 POPPERS

10 to 12 fresh jalapeño peppers*

1 package (8 ounces) cream cheese, softened

1½ cups (6 ounces) shredded Cheddar cheese, divided

2 green onions, finely chopped

½ teaspoon onion powder

¼ teaspoon salt

⅛ teaspoon garlic powder

6 slices bacon, crisp-cooked and finely chopped

2 tablespoons panko bread crumbs

2 tablespoons grated Parmesan or Romano cheese

*For large jalapeño peppers, use 10. For small peppers, use 12.

1. Cut each jalapeño pepper** in half lengthwise; remove ribs and seeds.

2. Combine cream cheese, 1 cup Cheddar cheese, green onions, onion powder, salt and garlic powder in medium bowl. Stir in bacon. Fill each pepper half with about 1 tablespoon cheese mixture. Sprinkle with remaining ½ cup Cheddar cheese, panko and Parmesan cheese.

3. Preheat air fryer to 370°F. Line basket with parchment paper or foil.

4. Cook 5 to 7 minutes or until cheese is melted and browned but peppers are still firm.

**Jalapeño peppers can sting and irritate the skin, so wear rubber gloves when handling peppers and do not touch your eyes.

WARM GOAT CHEESE ROUNDS

MAKES 4 SERVINGS

1 **package (4 ounces) garlic herb goat cheese**

1 **egg**

1 **tablespoon water**

⅓ **cup seasoned dry bread crumbs**

Marinara sauce, heated

1. Cut cheese crosswise into 8 slices. (If cheese is too difficult to slice, shape scant tablespoonfuls of cheese into balls and flatten into ¼-inch-thick rounds.)

2. Beat egg and water in small bowl. Place bread crumbs in shallow dish. Dip cheese rounds into egg mixture, then in bread crumbs, turning to coat all sides. Gently press bread crumbs to adhere. Place coated rounds on plate; freeze 10 minutes.

3. Preheat air fryer to 370°F. Cook in batches 10 minutes, flipping halfway through cooking, until golden brown. Serve immediately with marinara sauce.

PEPPERONI BREAD

MAKES ABOUT 6 SERVINGS

1 package (about 14 ounces) refrigerated pizza dough

8 slices provolone cheese

20 to 30 slices pepperoni (about ½ of 6-ounce package)

¾ cup (3 ounces) shredded mozzarella cheese

½ cup grated Parmesan cheese

½ teaspoon Italian seasoning

1 egg, beaten

Marinara sauce, heated

1. Unroll pizza dough on lightly floured surface; cut dough in half.

2. Working with one half at a time, arrange half the provolone slices on half the dough. Top with half the pepperoni, half the mozzarella and Parmesan cheeses and half the Italian seasoning. Repeat with other half dough and toppings.

3. Fold top half of dough over filling; press edges with fork or pinch edges to seal.

4. Preheat air fryer to 390°F. Line basket with parchment paper. Transfer one bread to basket. Brush with egg.

5. Cook 8 to 10 minutes or until crust is golden brown. Remove to wire rack to cool slightly. Repeat with other bread. Cut crosswise into slices; serve warm with marinara sauce.

GARLIC BITES

MAKES 24 APPETIZERS

½ **of 16-ounce package frozen phyllo dough, thawed to room temperature**

¾ **cup (1½ sticks) butter, melted**

3 **large heads garlic, separated into cloves, peeled**

½ **cup finely chopped walnuts**

1 **cup Italian-style bread crumbs**

1. Remove phyllo from package; unroll and place on large sheet of waxed paper. Cut phyllo crosswise into 2-inch-wide strips. Cover phyllo with large sheet of plastic wrap and damp, clean kitchen towel. (Phyllo dries out quickly if not covered.)

2. Lay 1 strip of phyllo at a time on flat surface; brush immediately with butter. Place 1 clove of garlic at end. Sprinkle 1 teaspoon walnuts along length of strip.

3. Roll up garlic clove and walnuts in strip, tucking in side edges as you roll. Brush with butter; roll in bread crumbs. Repeat with remaining phyllo, garlic, walnuts, butter and bread crumbs.

4. Preheat air fryer to 350°F. Line basket with parchment paper. Cook in batches 6 to 8 minutes or until golden brown. Cool slightly.

PIGGIES IN A BASKET

MAKES 4 SERVINGS

1 package (8 ounces) refrigerated crescent roll dough

1 package (about 12 ounces) cocktail franks

1. Cut crescent dough into strips. Wrap dough around each frank.

2. Preheat air fryer to 350°F.

3. Cook in batches 3 to 4 minutes or until golden brown.

PORKY PINWHEELS

MAKES 24 PINWHEELS

1   **sheet frozen puff pastry (half of a 17¼-ounce package), thawed**

1   **egg white, beaten**

8   **slices bacon, crisp-cooked and crumbled**

2   **tablespoons packed brown sugar**

¼   **teaspoon ground red pepper**

---

1. Place pastry on sheet of parchment paper. Brush with egg white.

2. Combine bacon, brown sugar and ground red pepper in small bowl. Sprinkle evenly over top of pastry; press lightly to adhere. Roll pastry jelly-roll style from long end. Wrap in parchment paper. Refrigerate 30 minutes.

3. Preheat air fryer to 370°F. Line basket with parchment paper. Slice pastry into ½-inch-thick slices.

4. Cook in batches 8 to 10 minutes or until light golden brown. Remove to wire racks; cool completely.

EVERYTHING SEASONING DIP WITH BAGEL CHIPS

MAKES 2 CUPS DIP (ABOUT 16 SERVINGS)

2 large bagels, sliced vertically into rounds

1 container (12 ounces) whipped cream cheese

1½ tablespoons green onion, finely chopped (green part only)

1 teaspoon dried minced onion

1 teaspoon granulated garlic

1 teaspoon sesame seeds

1 teaspoon poppy seeds

¼ teaspoon kosher salt

1. Preheat air fryer to 350°F.

2. Coat bagel rounds generously with butter-flavored nonstick cooking spray. Cook 7 to 8 minutes, shaking occasionally, until golden brown.

3. Meanwhile, combine cream cheese, green onion, minced onion, garlic, sesame seeds, poppy seeds and salt in medium bowl until well blended.

4. Serve chips with dip.

SUPER SALAMI TWISTS

MAKES 12 SERVINGS

1 **egg**

1 **tablespoon milk**

1 **cup (about ¼ pound) finely chopped hard salami**

2 **tablespoons yellow cornmeal**

1 **teaspoon Italian seasoning**

1 **package (about 11 ounces) refrigerated breadstick dough (12 breadsticks)**

¾ **cup pasta sauce, heated**

1. Beat egg and milk in shallow dish until well blended. Combine salami, cornmeal and Italian seasoning in separate shallow dish.

2. Unroll breadstick dough. Separate into 12 pieces along perforations. Roll each piece of dough in egg mixture, then in salami mixture, gently pressing salami into dough. Twist each piece of dough twice.

3. Preheat air fryer to 370°F. Line basket with parchment paper.

4. Cook in batches 8 to 10 minutes or until golden brown. Remove to wire rack; cool 5 minutes. Serve warm with pasta sauce for dipping.

CAPRESE-STYLE TARTLETS

MAKES 6 TARTLETS

3 tomatoes, cut into 4 slices each

3 tablespoons prepared pesto

1 sheet frozen puff pastry (half of 17¼-ounce package)

6 ounces fresh mozzarella cheese

2 tablespoons chopped kalamata olives

1. Place tomatoes in large resealable food storage bag. Add pesto; toss to coat. Marinate at room temperature 30 minutes.

2. Unfold puff pastry; thaw 20 minutes on lightly floured surface.

3. Preheat air fryer to 370°F. Line basket with parchment paper.

4. Cut out 6 (4-inch) rounds from pastry. Top each round with 2 tomato slices. Cook in batches 8 to 10 minutes or until pastry is light golden and puffed.

5. Cut cheese into 6 (¼-inch-thick) slices. Top each tart with 1 cheese slice. Cook in batches 1 minute or until cheese is melted. Top tarts evenly with olives. Serve warm.

BACON-WRAPPED TERIYAKI SHRIMP

MAKES 6 SERVINGS

1 **pound large raw shrimp, peeled and deveined (with tails on)**

¼ **cup teriyaki marinade**

12 **slices bacon, cut in half crosswise**

1. Place shrimp in large resealable food storage bag. Add teriyaki marinade; seal bag and turn to coat. Marinate in refrigerator 15 to 20 minutes.

2. Remove shrimp from bag; reserve marinade. Wrap each shrimp with 1 piece bacon. Brush bacon with some of reserved marinade.

3. Preheat air fryer to 390°F. Line basket with parchment paper or foil; spray lightly with nonstick cooking spray.

4. Cook 4 to 6 minutes or until bacon is crisp and shrimp are pink and opaque.

TIP: Do not use thick-cut bacon for this recipe, because the bacon will not be completely cooked when the shrimp are cooked through.

CITRUS CANDIED NUTS

MAKES ABOUT 3 CUPS

1 egg white
1½ cups whole almonds
1½ cups pecan halves
1 cup powdered sugar
2 tablespoons lemon juice

2 teaspoons grated orange peel
1 teaspoon grated lemon peel
⅛ teaspoon ground nutmeg

1. Beat egg white in medium bowl with electric mixer at high speed until soft peaks form. Add almonds and pecans; stir until well coated. Stir in powdered sugar, lemon juice, orange peel, lemon peel and nutmeg until evenly coated.

2. Preheat air fryer to 350°F. Spray basket with nonstick cooking spray.

3. Cook 6 to 8 minutes, stirring and shaking several times during cooking, until nuts are lightly browned. Remove nuts to bowl or tray to cool. Cool completely. Store in airtight container up to 2 weeks.

SPEEDY SALAMI SPIRALS

MAKES ABOUT 28 SPIRALS

1 **package (about 14 ounces) refrigerated pizza dough**

1 **cup (4 ounces) shredded Italian cheese blend**

3 **to 4 ounces thinly sliced Genoa salami**

---

1. Unroll dough on cutting board or clean work surface; press into 15×10-inch rectangle. Sprinkle evenly with cheese; top with salami.

2. Starting with long side, tightly roll up dough and filling jelly-roll style, pinching seam to seal. Cut roll crosswise into ½-inch slices. (If roll is too soft to cut, refrigerate or freeze until firm.)

3. Preheat air fryer to 390°F. Line basket with parchment paper.

4. Cook in batches 8 to 10 minutes or until golden brown. Serve warm.

AIR-FRIED PARMESAN PICKLE CHIPS

MAKES 8 SERVINGS

- **4 large whole dill pickles**
- **½ cup all-purpose flour**
- **½ teaspoon salt**
- **2 eggs**
- **½ cup panko bread crumbs**

- **2 tablespoons grated Parmesan cheese**
- **½ cup garlic aioli mayonnaise or ranch dressing**

1. Line baking sheet with paper towels. Slice pickles diagonally into ¼-inch slices; place on prepared baking sheet. Pat dry on top with paper towels to remove any moisture from pickles.

2. Combine flour and salt in shallow dish. Beat eggs in another shallow dish. Combine panko and Parmesan cheese in third shallow dish.

3. Coat pickles in flour. Dip in eggs, letting excess drip back into dish, then coat evenly with panko.

4. Preheat air fryer to 390°F. Cook in batches 8 to 10 minutes or until golden brown. Remove carefully. Serve with aioli or dressing.

GRILLED CHEESE KABOBS

MAKES 12 SERVINGS

12 thick slices whole wheat bread

3 thick slices sharp Cheddar cheese

3 thick slices Monterey Jack or Colby Jack cheese

2 tablespoons butter, melted

1. Cut each slice bread into 1-inch squares. Cut each slice cheese into 1-inch squares. Make small sandwiches with one square of bread and one square of each type of cheese. Top with second square of bread. Brush sandwiches with butter.

2. Preheat air fryer to 370°F. Cook sandwich squares 30 seconds to 1 minute or until golden brown and cheese is slightly melted.

MINI PEPPER NACHOS

MAKES 40 PEPPER HALVES (2 PER SERVING)

1 cup frozen corn, thawed

1 can (about 15 ounces) black beans, rinsed and drained

½ cup chopped tomatoes

½ teaspoon salt

20 mini sweet peppers, assorted colors, cut in half lengthwise and seeded

½ cup (2 ounces) shredded Mexican-style taco shredded cheese

½ cup sour cream (optional)

1 small avocado, chopped (optional)

2 tablespoons chopped green onion or cilantro (optional)

1. Combine corn, beans, tomatoes and salt in medium bowl. Fill peppers with about 1 tablespoon mixture. Sprinkle with cheese.

2. Preheat air fryer to 370°F. Line basket with foil. Cook 5 to 7 minutes or until cheese is lightly browned and melted. Remove to serving plate.

3. Top with sour cream, avocado and green onion, if desired.

GARLIC-HERB PARMESAN DIPPING STICKS

MAKES 12 SERVINGS

1 package (about 14 ounces) refrigerated pizza dough

¾ cup light garlic-and-herb spreadable cheese

¾ cup (3 ounces) shredded Italian cheese blend

¼ cup grated Parmesan cheese

½ teaspoon dried oregano

Warm marinara sauce and/or ranch salad dressing (optional)

1. Roll out dough on lightly floured surface to 12-inch square. Spread garlic-and-herb spreadable cheese evenly over bread. Top with cheese blend, Parmesan cheese and oregano.

2. Preheat air fryer to 390°F. Line basket with parchment paper; spray with nonstick cooking spray.

3. Cut dough in half or thirds to fit into basket. Cook in batches 6 to 8 minutes or until golden brown. Let cool slightly.

4. Slice lengthwise into strips. Serve with marinara sauce or salad dressing for dipping, if desired.

MINI CHICKPEA CAKES

MAKES 2 DOZEN CAKES (ABOUT 8 SERVINGS)

1 **can (about 15 ounces) chickpeas, rinsed and drained**

1 **cup grated carrots**

⅓ **cup seasoned dry bread crumbs**

¼ **cup creamy Italian salad dressing, plus additional for dipping**

1 **egg**

1. Coarsely mash chickpeas in medium bowl with fork or potato masher. Stir in carrots, bread crumbs, ¼ cup salad dressing and egg; mix well.

2. Shape chickpea mixture into 24 patties, using about 1 tablespoon mixture for each.

3. Preheat air fryer to 370°F. Spray basket with nonstick cooking spray.

4. Cook in batches 10 minutes, turning halfway through cooking, until lightly browned. Serve warm with additional salad dressing for dipping, if desired.

QUICK & EASY BREAKFASTS

BREAKFAST FLATS

MAKES 4 SERVINGS

1 package (about 14 ounces) refrigerated pizza dough

1½ cups (6 ounces) shredded Cheddar cheese

8 slices bacon, crisp-cooked and diced (optional)

4 eggs, fried

Kosher salt and black pepper (optional)

1. Divide pizza dough into 4 equal portions. Roll out on lightly floured surface into rectangles roughly 8½×4 inches. Top each evenly with cheese and bacon, if desired.

2. Preheat air fryer to 370°F. Line basket with parchment paper.

3. Cook in batches 5 to 7 minutes or until crust is golden brown and crisp and cheese is melted.

4. Top baked flats with fried egg; season with salt and pepper, if desired. Serve warm.

QUICK JELLY-FILLED BISCUIT DOUGHNUT BALLS

MAKES 20 DOUGHNUT BALLS

1 **package (about 7 ounces) refrigerated reduced-fat biscuit dough (10 biscuits)**

¼ **cup coarse sugar**

1 **cup strawberry preserves***

*If preserves are very chunky, process in food processor 10 seconds or press through fine-mesh sieve.

1. Preheat air fryer to 370°F.

2. Separate biscuits into 10 portions. Cut each in half; roll dough into balls to create 20 balls.

3. Cook in batches 5 to 6 minutes or until golden brown.

4. Place sugar in large bowl. Coat warm balls in sugar. Let cool. Using a piping bag with medium star tip; fill bag with preserves. Poke hole in side of each doughnut ball with paring knife; fill with preserves. Serve immediately.

CRUNCHY FRENCH TOAST STICKS

MAKES 6 SERVINGS

6 slices Italian bread (each 1 inch thick, about 3½ to 4 inches in diameter)

4 cups cornflake cereal, crushed

3 eggs

⅔ cup reduced-fat (2%) milk

1 tablespoon sugar

1 teaspoon vanilla

1 teaspoon ground cinnamon, plus additional for serving

¼ teaspoon ground nutmeg

1 container (6 ounces) vanilla yogurt

¼ cup maple syrup

1. Remove crusts from bread, if desired. Cut each bread slice into 3 strips. Place cornflake crumbs on waxed paper.

2. Whisk eggs, milk, sugar, vanilla, 1 teaspoon cinnamon and nutmeg in shallow dish. Dip bread strips in egg mixture, turning to generously coat all sides. Roll in cornflakes, coating all sides.

3. Preheat air fryer to 370°F. Cook in batches 8 to 10 minutes, turning halfway through cooking or until golden brown.

4. Meanwhile, combine yogurt and maple syrup in small bowl. Sprinkle with additional cinnamon, if desired. Serve French toast sticks with yogurt mixture.

CINNAMINI BUNS

MAKES 2 DOZEN

2 tablespoons packed
   brown sugar

½ teaspoon ground
   cinnamon

1 package (8 ounces)
   refrigerated crescent
   roll dough

1 tablespoon butter, melted

½ cup powdered sugar

1 to 1½ tablespoons milk

1. Combine brown sugar and cinnamon in small bowl; mix well.

2. Unroll dough and separate into 2 (12×4-inch) rectangles; firmly press perforations to seal. Brush dough with butter; sprinkle with brown sugar mixture. Starting with long side, roll up tightly jelly-roll style; pinch seams to seal. Cut each roll crosswise into 12 (1-inch) slices with serrated knife.

3. Preheat air fryer to 370°F. Line basket with parchment paper.

4. Cook, seam side up, in batches 5 to 7 minutes or until golden brown. Remove to wire rack; cool.

5. Combine powdered sugar and 1 tablespoon milk in small bowl; whisk until smooth. Add additional milk, 1 teaspoon at a time, to reach desired glaze consistency. Drizzle glaze over buns.

RASPBERRY PUFFS

MAKES 8 PUFFS

1 package (8 ounces) refrigerated crescent roll dough

¼ cup raspberry fruit spread

½ of an 8-ounce package cream cheese, softened

1 to 2 teaspoons sugar

2 tablespoons reduced-fat (2%) milk

¼ teaspoon vanilla

1. Separate crescent roll dough into 8 triangles; unroll on lightly floured surface. Brush 1½ teaspoons fruit spread evenly over each roll. Roll up each triangle, starting at wide end.

2. Preheat air fryer to 370°F. Line basket with parchment paper.

3. Cook in batches 5 to 6 minutes or until lightly golden. Cool.

4. Meanwhile, whisk together cream cheese, sugar, milk and vanilla in small bowl until smooth. Spoon about 1 tablespoon cream cheese mixture over each cooled roll or serve on the side, as desired.

VARIATION: For an even lighter-tasting roll, replace the cream cheese mixture with powdered sugar. Simply sprinkle 2 tablespoons evenly over all.

OMELET CROISSANTS

MAKES 2 SERVINGS

2 large croissants

2 large eggs

¼ cup chopped mushrooms

¼ tablespoon chopped red and/or green bell pepper

Pinch of salt and black pepper

¼ cup (1 ounce) shredded Cheddar cheese

---

1. Cut slit across top of each croissant; using hands break open to separate.

2. Whisk eggs in small bowl. Add mushrooms, bell pepper, salt and black pepper. Spoon mixture equally in croissant opening. Sprinkle cheese over top.

3. Preheat air fryer to 330°F. Place croissants in parchment paper-lined basket.

4. Cook 12 to 15 minutes or until croissants are browned and eggs are set.

MAKE AHEAD: Prepared croissants can be stored in refrigerator for up to 3 days or in freezer for 1 month.

APPLE-CRANBERRY TURNOVERS

MAKES 4 TURNOVERS

1 sheet frozen puff pastry (half of a 17¼-ounce package), thawed

FILLING

1 large Granny Smith apple (about 7 ounces), peeled and diced (about 1 cup)

2 tablespoons dried cranberries

2 tablespoons packed dark brown sugar

1 tablespoon butter

¼ teaspoon ground cinnamon

⅛ teaspoon ground allspice

TOPPING

1½ teaspoons granulated sugar

⅛ teaspoon ground cinnamon

1 tablespoon butter, melted

1. Unfold puff pastry.

2. Place filling ingredients in medium saucepan. Cook and stir 2 to 3 minutes over medium heat until apples start to soften. Remove from heat; cool completely.

3. Cut pastry into 4 squares. Brush edges with water. Spoon ¼ cup of the apple mixture in center of each square and fold to create a triangle. Seal edges by pinching seams with fork. Place on baking sheet. Cover and refrigerate 30 minutes.

4. Preheat air fryer to 370°F. Remove turnovers from refrigerator. Make small cut on top of each turnover. Cook in batches 8 to 10 minutes or until puffed and golden brown.

5. For topping, combine granulated sugar and ⅛ teaspoon cinnamon in small bowl. Brush equal amounts of butter on each warm turnover; sprinkle with cinnamon-sugar mixture. Serve warm or at room temperature.

QUICK CHOCOLATE CHIP STICKY BUNS

MAKES ABOUT 12 STICKY BUNS

1 package (about 11 ounces) refrigerated French bread dough

¼ cup sugar

1 teaspoon ground cinnamon

½ cup mini semisweet chocolate chips

2 tablespoons butter

⅓ cup chopped pecans, toasted*

1 tablespoon maple syrup

To toast nuts, cook in preheated 325°F parchment paper-lined air fryer 3 to 4 minutes or until golden brown.

1. Unroll dough on lightly floured large cutting board or clean work surface. Combine sugar and cinnamon in small bowl; sprinkle evenly over dough. Top with chocolate chips. Starting with short side, roll up dough jelly-roll style. Cut crosswise into 12 (¾-inch) slices with serrated knife.

2. Combine butter, pecans and maple syrup in small bowl; mix well.

3. Preheat air fryer to 370°F. Line basket with parchment paper; spray with nonstick cooking spray.

4. Arrange dough slices cut sides up in basket, brush butter mixture over top of rolls. Cook 8 to 10 minutes or until golden brown. Serve warm.

CAULIFLOWER "HASH BROWN" PATTIES

MAKES 8 SERVINGS

4 slices bacon

1 package (about 12 ounces) cauliflower rice

½ cup finely chopped onion

½ cup finely chopped red and/or green bell pepper

1 large egg

⅓ cup all-purpose flour

½ cup (2 ounces) shredded Cheddar cheese

1 tablespoon chopped fresh chives

1 teaspoon salt

½ teaspoon black pepper

1. Preheat air fryer to 400°F. Cook bacon 8 to 10 minutes. Remove from basket to paper towels; blot any grease from bacon. Crumble into small pieces.

2. Place cauliflower in large bowl. Add bacon, onion, bell pepper, egg, flour, cheese, chives, salt and black pepper; mix well. Shape mixture into patties; place on baking sheet. Freeze 30 minutes.

3. Preheat air fryer to 370°F. Spray basket with nonstick cooking spray. Cook 12 to 15 minutes or until browned.

HOMEMADE AIR-FRIED BAGELS

MAKES 4 SERVINGS

1 **cup self-rising flour**
1 **cup plain nonfat Greek yogurt**
1 **large egg, beaten**

Sesame seeds, poppy seeds, dried onion flakes, everything bagel seasoning (optional)

Cream cheese or butter (optional)

---

1. Combine flour and yogurt in bowl of electric stand mixer with dough hook.* Beat 2 to 3 minutes or until mixture is well combined. Place dough on lightly floured surface; knead by hand about 4 to 5 minutes or until dough is smooth and elastic. Form dough into a ball.

2. Cut into 4 equal portions. Roll each into a ball. Pull and stretch dough to create desired shape, inserting finger into center to create hole. Repeat with remaining dough.

3. Preheat air fryer to 330°F. Line basket with parchment paper. Place bagels on parchment; brush with beaten egg. Sprinkle with desired toppings. Cook 8 to 10 minutes or until lightly browned.

4. Serve with cream cheese or butter, if desired.

Or, use heavy spatula in large bowl to combine mixture.

EASY RASPBERRY-PEACH DANISH

MAKES 8 SERVINGS

1 package (8 ounces) refrigerated crescent dough sheet

¼ cup raspberry fruit spread

1 can (about 15 ounces) sliced peaches in juice, drained and chopped

1 egg white, beaten

½ cup powdered sugar

2 to 3 teaspoons orange juice

¼ cup chopped pecans, toasted*

To toast nuts, cook in preheated 325°F parchment paper-lined air fryer 3 to 4 minutes or until golden brown.

1. Place dough on lightly floured surface; cut in half. Roll each half into 12×8-inch rectangle.

2. Spread half of raspberry spread along center of each dough rectangle; top with peaches. Make 2-inch-long cuts from edges towards filling on long sides of each dough rectangle at 1-inch intervals. Fold strips of dough over filling. Brush with egg white.

3. Preheat air fryer to 370°F. Line basket with parchment paper. Cook each half 5 to 7 minutes or until golden brown. Remove to wire rack; cool slightly.

4. Combine powdered sugar and enough orange juice in small bowl to make pourable glaze. Drizzle glaze over danish; sprinkle with pecans.

APPLE BUTTER ROLLS

MAKES 12 SERVINGS

1 **package (about 11 ounces) refrigerated breadstick dough (12 breadsticks)**

2 **tablespoons apple butter**

¼ **cup sifted powdered sugar**

1 **to 1½ teaspoons orange juice**

¼ **teaspoon grated orange peel (optional)**

---

1. Unroll breadstick dough; separate into 12 pieces along perforations. Gently stretch each piece to 9 inches in length. Twist ends of each piece in opposite directions three or four times. Coil each twisted strip into snail shape; tuck ends underneath. Use thumb to make small indentation in center of each breadstick coil. Spoon about ½ teaspoon apple butter into each indentation.

2. Preheat air fryer to 370°F. Line basket with parchment paper; spray with nonstick cooking spray.

3. Cook in batches 8 to 10 minutes or until golden brown. Remove to wire rack; cool 10 minutes.

4. Meanwhile, combine powdered sugar and 1 teaspoon orange juice in small bowl; whisk until smooth. Add additional orange juice, if necessary, to make pourable glaze. Stir in orange peel, if desired. Drizzle glaze over rolls. Serve warm.

AIR-FRIED OMELET SCRAMBLE

MAKES 2 SERVINGS

2 large eggs
2 tablespoons milk
¼ teaspoon salt
⅛ teaspoon black pepper
2 tablespoons chopped red and/or green bell pepper

2 tablespoons chopped onion
¼ cup (1 ounce) shredded Cheddar cheese, divided

1. Spray 6×3-inch baking dish or 2 small ramekins* with nonstick cooking spray.

2. Whisk eggs, milk, salt and black pepper in medium bowl. Add bell pepper, onion and 2 tablespoons cheese. Pour into prepared dish.

3. Preheat air fryer to 350°F. Cook 10 to 12 minutes, slightly breaking up eggs after 5 minutes. Top with remaining cheese.

Depending on the size of your air fryer, you may need to modify the size of the baking dish.

BROILED GRAPEFRUIT YOUR WAY

MAKES 2 SERVINGS

1 large pink grapefruit

2 teaspoons honey

2 teaspoons packed brown sugar

1. Cut grapefruit in half horizontally. Use a sharp knife to cut around edges and sections of grapefruit where the rind meets the fruit.

2. Drizzle each half with honey; sprinkle with brown sugar.

3. Preheat air fryer to 400°F. Cook 5 to 7 minutes until lightly browned and bubbly.

VARIATION: Sprinkle grapefruit with cinnamon-sugar mixture or toasted coconut instead of honey and brown sugar.

STRAWBERRY CHEESE DANISHES

MAKES 8 SERVINGS

½ **cup cream cheese,**
  softened

2 **tablespoons granulated**
  sugar

2 **teaspoons lemon juice**

½ **teaspoon grated lemon**
  peel

1 **package (8 ounces)**
  refrigerated crescent
  roll dough

8 **teaspoons strawberry**
  preserves

  Powdered sugar (optional)

1. Combine cream cheese, granulated sugar, lemon juice and lemon peel in small bowl.

2. Separate dough into 4 rectangles; press perforations to seal. Working with one piece of dough at a time, spread each rectangle with 2 tablespoons cream cheese mixture. Roll up lengthwise, pinching edge and ends to seal. Carefully stretch each roll to about 12 inches. Cut each in half.

3. Shape halves into spirals, tucking ends under. Make indentation in center of each roll; fill with 1 teaspoon preserves.

4. Preheat air fryer to 370°F. Cook in batches 5 to 7 minutes or until lightly browned. Remove to wire rack. Cool slightly. Sprinkle rolls with powdered sugar, if desired.

VARIATION: Any flavor preserves may be used in place of the strawberry preserves.

BREAKFAST PEPPERONI FLATBREAD

MAKES 2 SERVINGS

1 flatbread
½ cup (2 ounces) shredded mozzarella cheese
1 plum tomato, diced

12 slices turkey pepperoni, cut into quarters
1 teaspoon grated Parmesan cheese
¼ cup chopped fresh basil

1. Place flatbread on parchment paper. Sprinkle with mozzarella cheese, tomatoes, pepperoni and Parmesan cheese.

2. Preheat air fryer to 370°F.

3. Cook 3 to 5 minutes or until cheese is melted. Sprinkle with basil. Cool slightly before cutting.

FRENCH TOAST STICKS

MAKES 4 SERVINGS

4 eggs
⅓ cup reduced-fat (2%) milk
1 teaspoon ground cinnamon
1 teaspoon vanilla

4 slices Italian bread, cut into 3 portions each
1 teaspoon powdered sugar
¼ cup maple syrup

1. Combine eggs, milk, cinnamon and vanilla in large shallow dish.

2. Dip bread sticks in egg mixture to coat.

3. Preheat air fryer to 370°F. Line basket with parchment paper; spray with nonstick cooking spray.

4. Cook in batches 8 to 10 minutes or until golden brown. Dust lightly with powdered sugar; serve with maple syrup.

RASPBERRY WHITE CHOCOLATE DANISH

MAKES 8 SERVINGS

1 **package (8 ounces) refrigerated crescent roll dough**

8 **teaspoons red raspberry preserves**

1 **ounce white baking chocolate, chopped**

1. Unroll crescent dough; separate into 8 triangles. Place 1 teaspoon preserves in center of each triangle. Fold right and left corners of long side over filling to top corner to form rectangle. Pinch edges to seal.

2. Preheat air fryer to 370°F. Line basket with parchment paper; spray with nonstick cooking spray.

3. Cook in batches, seam side up, 5 to 7 minutes or until lightly browned. Remove to wire rack to cool 5 minutes.

4. Place white chocolate in small resealable food storage bag. Microwave on MEDIUM (50%) 1 minute; gently knead bag. Microwave and knead at additional 30-second intervals until chocolate is completely melted. Cut off small corner of bag; drizzle chocolate over danish.

LUNCHES & SANDWICHES

PIZZA SANDWICH

MAKES 4 TO 6 SERVINGS

1 loaf (12 ounces) focaccia
½ cup pizza sauce
20 slices pepperoni
8 slices (1 ounce each) mozzarella cheese

1 can (2¼ ounces) sliced mushrooms, drained
Red pepper flakes (optional)
Olive oil

1. Cut focaccia horizontally in half.* Spread cut sides of both halves with pizza sauce. Layer bottom half with pepperoni, cheese and mushrooms; sprinkle with red pepper flakes, if desired. Cover with top half of focaccia. Brush sandwich lightly with oil.

2. Preheat air fryer to 370°F.

3. Cook 3 to 5 minutes or until cheese melts and bread is golden brown. Cut into wedges to serve.

Depending on the size of your air fryer, you may need to cut the focaccia vertically in half to fit.

NOTE: Focaccia can be found in the bakery section of most supermarkets. It is often available in different flavors, such as tomato, herb, cheese or onion.

TUNA PIES
MAKES 4 SERVINGS

1 package (8 ounces) refrigerated crescent dough sheet

1 can (about 5 ounces) water-packed tuna, drained

1 tablespoon mayonnaise

1 cup (4 ounces) shredded Cheddar cheese

1. Preheat air fryer to 370°F. Spray 4 ramekins with nonstick cooking spray.

2. Roll out dough onto lightly floured surface to 12×8-inch rectangle. Cut into 4 (6×4-inch) rectangles. Press dough into bottoms and up sides of prepared ramekins.

3. Combine tuna and mayonnaise in small bowl; mix gently. Spoon tuna mixture evenly over dough; sprinkle with cheese.

4. Cook in batches 8 to 10 minutes or until dough is golden brown. Let cool slightly before serving.

VARIATION: You can add vegetables, like broccoli, celery or peas, to this recipe, as well as trying other types of cheese, like mozzarella or Swiss.

SANDWICH MONSTERS

MAKES 7 SERVINGS

1 package (about 16 ounces) refrigerated jumbo buttermilk biscuits (8 biscuits)

1 cup (4 ounces) shredded mozzarella cheese

⅓ cup sliced mushrooms

2 ounces pepperoni slices (about 35 slices), quartered

½ cup pizza sauce, plus additional for serving

1 egg, beaten

1. Separate biscuits; set aside 1 biscuit for decoration. Roll out remaining biscuits into 7-inch circles on lightly floured surface.

2. Top half of each round evenly with cheese, mushrooms, pepperoni and ½ cup pizza sauce, leaving ½-inch border. Fold dough over filling to form semicircle; seal edges with fork. Brush tops with egg.

3. Split remaining biscuit horizontally; cut each half into 8 (¼-inch) strips. For each sandwich, roll 2 strips of dough into spirals for eyes. Divide remaining 2 strips of dough into 7 pieces for noses. Arrange eyes and noses on tops of sandwiches; brush with egg.

4. Preheat air fryer to 370°F. Line basket with parchment paper or foil.

5. Cook in batches 6 to 8 minutes or until golden brown. Remove to wire rack; cool 5 minutes. Serve with additional pizza sauce.

TIP: Don't worry about leaking sauce or cheese—it will look like it's coming from the monster's mouth!

BAKED SALAMI

MAKES 5 SERVINGS

1 all-beef kosher salami
(14 to 16 ounces)

½ cup apricot preserves

1 tablespoon hot pepper
sauce

2 tablespoons packed
brown sugar

Bread slices

1. Peel off plastic wrap of salami. Cut 12 crosswise (½-inch-deep) slits across top. Place, cut side up, in small dish that fits inside air fryer.

2. Combine preserves, hot pepper sauce and brown sugar in small bowl; stir well. Spoon sauce over top.

3. Preheat air fryer to 370°F. Cook 8 to 10 minutes or until juicy and dark brown, spooning sauce over salami occasionally during cooking.

4. Cut salami into thin slices; toss with sauce. Serve on bread.

EXTRAS: Serve with slices of challah bread or cocktail rye.

BACON-TOMATO GRILLED CHEESE

MAKES 2 SERVINGS

4 slices bacon, cut in half

2 slices sharp Cheddar
    cheese

2 slices Gouda cheese

2 slices tomato

4 slices whole wheat or
    white bread

1. Preheat air fryer to 400°F. Cook bacon 8 to 10 minutes. Remove from basket to paper towels; blot any grease from bacon.

2. Meanwhile, layer 1 slice Cheddar cheese, 1 slice Gouda cheese, 1 slice tomato and 2 slices bacon between 2 bread slices. Repeat with remaining ingredients.

3. Reduce heat on air fryer to 350°F. Cook 3 to 5 minutes or until cheese is melted and bread is golden brown.

AIR-FRIED PEPPERONI PIZZA BAGELS

MAKES 4 SERVINGS

4 **Homemade Air-Fried Bagels (recipe on page 72) or store-bought bagels**

¼ **cup marinara sauce**

¼ **cup mini pepperoni slices**

¼ **cup (1 ounce) shredded mozzarella cheese**

Dried oregano

1. Cut bagels in half lengthwise. Top each half with equal amount sauce, pepperoni and cheese.

2. Preheat air fryer to 350°F. Line basket with foil or parchment paper. Cook 3 to 5 minutes or until cheese is melted and browned. Sprinkle with oregano.

SPINACH & ROASTED PEPPER PANINI

MAKES 6 TO 8 SERVINGS

1   loaf (12 ounces) focaccia

1½ cups spinach leaves
    (about 12 leaves)

1   jar (about 7 ounces)
    roasted red peppers,
    drained

4   ounces fontina cheese,
    thinly sliced

¾   cup thinly sliced red onion

    Olive oil (optional)

1. Cut focaccia horizontally in half.* Layer bottom half with spinach, roasted peppers, cheese and onion. Cover with top half of focaccia. Brush outsides of sandwich lightly with oil, if desired.

2. Preheat air fryer to 370°F. Line basket with parchment paper. Cook in batches 3 to 5 minutes or until cheese melts and bread is golden brown.

Depending on the size of your air fryer, you may need to cut the focaccia vertically in half to fit.

NOTE: Focaccia can be found in the bakery section of most supermarkets. It is often available in different flavors, such as tomato, herb, cheese or onion.

TASTY TURKEY TURNOVERS
MAKES 6 SERVINGS

1 package (about 8 ounces) refrigerated crescent roll sheet

2 tablespoons honey mustard, plus additional for serving

3 ounces thinly sliced lean deli turkey breast

¾ cup packaged broccoli coleslaw mix

1 egg white, beaten

1. Roll out dough onto lightly floured surface. Using a wide glass or cookie cutter, cut into 3½-inch circles. Spread 2 tablespoons honey mustard lightly over dough circles; top with turkey and coleslaw mix. Brush edges of dough with egg white. Fold circles in half; press edges with tines of fork to seal. Brush with egg white.

2. Preheat air fryer to 370°F. Spray basket with nonstick cooking spray.

3. Cook in batches 6 to 7 minutes or until golden brown. Let stand 5 minutes before serving. Serve warm or at room temperature with additional honey mustard for dipping, if desired.

BELL PEPPER AND RICOTTA CALZONES

MAKES 6 SERVINGS

2 teaspoons olive oil

1 medium red bell pepper, diced

1 medium green bell pepper, diced

1 small onion, diced

½ teaspoon Italian seasoning

⅛ teaspoon black pepper

1 clove garlic, minced

1¼ cups marinara sauce, divided

¼ cup part-skim ricotta cheese

⅛ cup part-skim mozzarella cheese

1 package (14 ounces) refrigerated pizza dough

1. Heat oil in medium nonstick skillet over medium heat. Add bell peppers, onion, Italian seasoning and black pepper. Cook about 8 minutes, stirring occasionally until vegetables are tender. Add garlic, and cook 1 minute, stirring constantly. Stir in ½ cup marinara sauce; cook about 2 minutes or until thickened slightly. Transfer vegetable mixture to plate; let cool slightly.

2. Combine ricotta and mozzarella cheeses in small bowl; mix well. Unroll pizza dough and cut into 6 (4-inch) squares. Pat each square into 5-inch square. Spoon ⅓ cup vegetable mixture into center of each square; sprinkle with 1 tablespoon cheese mixture. Fold dough over filling to form triangle; pinch and fold edges together to seal.

3. Preheat air fryer to 370°F. Line basket with parchment paper.

4. Cook in batches 8 to 10 minutes or until lightly browned. Cool 5 minutes. Serve with remaining marinara sauce.

VEGGIE PIZZA PITAS

MAKES 2 SERVINGS

1 whole wheat pita bread round, cut in half horizontally (to make 2 rounds)

2 tablespoons pizza sauce

½ teaspoon dried basil

⅛ teaspoon red pepper flakes (optional)

½ cup sliced mushrooms

¼ cup thinly sliced green bell pepper

¼ cup thinly sliced red onion

½ cup (2 ounces) shredded mozzarella cheese

1 teaspoon grated Parmesan cheese

1. Arrange pita rounds, rough sides up, in single layer on parchment paper. Spread 1 tablespoon pizza sauce evenly over each round to within ¼ inch of edge. Sprinkle with basil and red pepper flakes, if desired. Top with mushrooms, bell pepper and onion. Sprinkle with mozzarella cheese.

2. Preheat air fryer to 370°F.

3. Cook in batches 5 to 7 minutes or until cheese melts. Sprinkle ½ teaspoon Parmesan cheese over each pita round.

NOTE: These pitas can be served as appetizers, as well.

CLASSIC GRILLED CHEESE
MAKES 2 SANDWICHES

4 slices (about ¾ ounce each) American cheese

4 slices white bread
   Butter, melted

1. Place 2 slices cheese each on 2 bread slices; top with remaining bread slices. Brush outsides of sandwiches with butter.

2. Preheat air fryer to 350°F. Cook in batches 3 to 5 minutes per side or until cheese melts and sandwiches are golden brown.

VEGETABLE AND HUMMUS MUFFALETTA

MAKES 8 SERVINGS

1 small eggplant, cut lengthwise into ⅛-inch slices

1 yellow squash, cut lengthwise into ⅛-inch slices

1 zucchini, cut on the diagonal into ⅛-inch slices

1 tablespoon extra virgin olive oil

¼ teaspoon salt

¼ teaspoon black pepper

1 boule or round bread (8 inches), cut in half horizontally

1 container (8 ounces) hummus, any flavor

1 jar (12 ounces) roasted red bell peppers, drained

1 jar (6 ounces) marinated artichoke hearts, drained and chopped

1 small tomato, thinly sliced

1. Combine eggplant, squash, zucchini, oil, salt and black pepper in large bowl; toss to coat.

2. Preheat air fryer to 390°F. Cook vegetables in batches 4 to 6 minutes, shaking halfway during cooking, until tender and golden. Cool to room temperature.

3. Scoop out bread from both halves of boule, leaving about 1 inch of bread on edges and about 1½ inches on bottom. (Reserve bread for bread crumbs or croutons.) Spread hummus evenly on inside bottom of bread. Layer vegetables, roasted peppers, artichokes and tomato over hummus; cover with top half of bread. Wrap stuffed loaf tightly in plastic wrap. Refrigerate at least 1 hour before cutting into wedges.

SUBSTITUTION: You can substitute a red bell pepper for the jarred peppers and roast it in the air fryer. Preheat air fryer to 390°F. Cook 15 minutes, turning once or twice. Let sit in air fryer 10 minutes longer to loosen skin. Carefully remove skin with paring knife.

TUNA MELTS

MAKES 2 SERVINGS

1 **can (about 5 ounces) chunk white tuna packed in water, drained and flaked**

½ **cup packaged coleslaw mix**

1 **tablespoon sliced green onion**

1 **tablespoon light mayonnaise**

½ **tablespoon Dijon mustard**

¼ **teaspoon dried dill weed (optional)**

2 **English muffins, split**

¼ **cup (1 ounce) shredded reduced-fat Cheddar cheese**

---

1. Combine tuna, coleslaw mix and green onion in medium bowl. Combine mayonnaise, mustard and dill weed, if desired, in small bowl. Stir mayonnaise mixture into tuna mixture. Spread tuna mixture onto muffin halves.

2. Preheat air fryer to 370°F. Cook 3 to 4 minutes or until heated through and lightly browned. Sprinkle with cheese. Cook 1 to 2 minutes or until cheese melts.

SALMON CROQUETTES

MAKES 5 SERVINGS (2 PER SERVING)

1 can (14¾ ounces) pink salmon, drained and flaked

½ cup mashed potatoes*

1 egg, beaten

3 tablespoons diced red bell pepper

2 tablespoons sliced green onion

1 tablespoon chopped fresh parsley

½ cup seasoned dry bread crumbs

Use mashed potatoes that are freshly made, leftover, or potatoes made from instant potatoes.

1. Combine salmon, potatoes, egg, bell pepper, green onion and parsley in medium bowl; mix well.

2. Place bread crumbs on medium plate. Shape salmon mixture into 10 croquettes about 3 inches long by 1 inch wide. Roll croquettes in bread crumbs to coat. Place on baking sheet. Refrigerate 15 to 20 minutes or until firm.

3. Preheat air fryer to 350°F. Cook in batches 6 to 8 minutes or until browned. Serve immediately.

MOZZARELLA & ROASTED RED PEPPER SANDWICH

MAKES 1 SERVING

- 1 tablespoon olive oil vinaigrette or Italian salad dressing
- 2 slices Italian-style sandwich bread (2 ounces)
- 2 fresh basil leaves
- ⅓ cup roasted red peppers, rinsed, drained and patted dry
- 1 to 2 slices (1 ounce each) part-skim mozzarella or Swiss cheese

1. Brush dressing on 1 side of 1 bread slice; top with basil, roasted peppers, cheese and remaining bread slice. Lightly spray both sides of sandwich with nonstick cooking spray.

2. Preheat air fryer to 350°F. Cook 4 to 5 minutes, turning halfway through cooking, until cheese melts and bread is golden brown.

PUNCHED PIZZA ROUNDS

MAKES 20 SERVINGS

1 package (12 ounces) refrigerated flaky buttermilk biscuits (10 biscuits)

1 package (5 ounces) mini pepperoni slices

¼ cup chopped bell pepper (optional)

1 tablespoon dried basil

½ cup pizza sauce

1½ cups (6 ounces) shredded mozzarella cheese

Shredded Parmesan cheese (optional)

1. Spray (2½-inch) silicone muffin cups with nonstick cooking spray.

2. Separate biscuits; split each biscuit in half horizontally to create 20 rounds. Place in prepared muffin cups. Press 4 pepperoni slices into center of each round. Sprinkle with bell pepper, if desired, and basil. Spread pizza sauce over pepperoni; sprinkle with mozzarella cheese.

3. Preheat air fryer to 370°F. Cook in batches 14 to 16 minutes or until pizzas are golden brown. Sprinkle with Parmesan cheese, if desired. Cool 2 minutes; remove to wire racks. Serve warm.

DELICIOUS DINNERS

FRIED BUTTERMILK CHICKEN FINGERS

MAKES 4 SERVINGS

CHICKEN

- 1½ cups biscuit baking mix (regular, not low-fat)
- 1 cup buttermilk*
- 1 egg, beaten
- 12 chicken tenders (about 1½ pounds), rinsed and patted dry

DIPPING SAUCE

- ⅓ cup mayonnaise
- 1 tablespoon honey
- 1 tablespoon prepared mustard
- 1 tablespoon packed dark brown sugar

If you don't have buttermilk, substitute 1 tablespoon vinegar or lemon juice plus enough milk to equal 1 cup. Let stand 5 minutes.

1. Place biscuit mix in pie pan or shallow dish. Combine buttermilk and egg in another shallow dish; mix until well blended.

2. Roll chicken pieces in biscuit mix, one at a time, coating evenly on all sides. Dip each chicken piece in buttermilk mixture; roll in biscuit mix again to coat evenly.

3. Preheat air fryer to 390°F. Cook in batches 10 to 12 minutes or until golden.

4. For dipping sauce, combine mayonnaise, honey, mustard and brown sugar in small bowl. Serve with chicken.

TERIYAKI SALMON

MAKES 2 SERVINGS

¼ cup dark sesame oil

Juice of 1 lemon

¼ cup soy sauce

2 tablespoons packed brown sugar

1 clove garlic, minced

2 salmon fillets (about 4 ounces each)

Hot cooked rice

Toasted sesame seeds and green onions (optional)

1. Whisk oil, lemon juice, soy sauce, brown sugar and garlic in medium bowl. Place salmon in large resealable food storage bag; add marinade. Refrigerate at least 2 hours.

2. Preheat air fryer to 350°F. Spray basket with nonstick cooking spray.

3. Cook 8 to 10 minutes or until salmon is crispy and easily flakes when tested with a fork. Serve with rice and garnish as desired.

BLUE CHEESE STUFFED CHICKEN BREASTS

MAKES 4 SERVINGS

- ½ **cup crumbled blue cheese**
- 2 **tablespoons butter, softened, divided**
- ¾ **teaspoon dried thyme**

- **Salt and black pepper**
- 4 **bone-in skin-on chicken breasts**
- 1 **tablespoon lemon juice**

1. Combine blue cheese, 1 tablespoon butter and thyme in small bowl; stir to blend. Season with salt and pepper.

2. Loosen chicken skin by pushing fingers between skin and meat, taking care not to tear skin. Spread cheese mixture under skin; massage skin to spread mixture evenly over chicken breast.

3. Melt remaining 1 tablespoon butter in small bowl; stir in lemon juice until blended. Brush mixture over chicken. Sprinkle with salt and pepper.

4. Preheat air fryer to 370°F. Cook 15 to 20 minutes or until chicken is cooked through.

BUTTERMILK AIR-FRIED CHICKEN

MAKES 4 SERVINGS

1 **cut-up whole chicken (2½ to 3 pounds)**

1 **cup buttermilk**

¾ **cup all-purpose flour**

½ **teaspoon salt**

½ **teaspoon ground red pepper**

¼ **teaspoon garlic powder**

2 **cups plain dry bread crumbs**

1. Place chicken pieces in large resealable food storage bag. Pour buttermilk over chicken. Close and refrigerate; let marinate at least 2 hours.

2. Combine flour, salt, red pepper and garlic powder in large shallow dish. Place bread crumbs in another shallow dish.

3. Preheat air fryer to 370°F. Spray basket with nonstick cooking spray.

4. Remove chicken pieces from buttermilk; coat with flour mixture then coat in bread crumbs. Spray chicken with cooking spray. Cook in batches 20 to 25 minutes or until brown and crisp on all sides and cooked through (165°F). Serve warm.

PARMESAN-CRUSTED TILAPIA

MAKES 6 SERVINGS

⅔ **cup plus 2 tablespoons grated Parmesan cheese, divided**

⅔ **cup panko bread crumbs**

⅓ **cup prepared light Alfredo sauce (refrigerated or jarred)**

1½ **teaspoons dried parsley flakes**

6 **tilapia fillets (4 ounces each)**

Shaved Parmesan cheese (optional)

Minced fresh parsley (optional)

1. Combine ⅔ cup grated Parmesan cheese and panko in medium bowl; mix well. Combine Alfredo sauce, remaining 2 tablespoons grated cheese and parsley flakes in small bowl; mix well. Spread Alfredo mixture over top of fish, coating in thick even layer. Top with panko mixture, pressing in gently to adhere.

2. Preheat air fryer to 390°F. Line basket with foil or parchment paper; spray with nonstick cooking spray.

3. Cook in batches 8 to 10 minutes or until crust is golden brown and fish begins to flake when tested with a fork. Garnish with shaved Parmesan cheese and fresh parsley.

LEMON-PEPPER CHICKEN

MAKES 4 SERVINGS

⅓ **cup lemon juice**

¼ **cup finely chopped onion**

2 **tablespoons olive oil**

1 **tablespoon packed brown sugar**

1 **tablespoon black pepper**

3 **cloves garlic, minced**

2 **teaspoons grated lemon peel**

½ **teaspoon salt**

4 **boneless skinless chicken breasts (about 1 pound)**

1. Combine lemon juice, onion, oil, brown sugar, pepper, garlic, lemon peel and salt in small bowl; stir to blend. Pour marinade over chicken in large resealable food storage bag. Seal bag; knead to coat. Refrigerate at least 4 hours or overnight.

2. Preheat air fryer to 370°F. Line basket with parchment paper or foil; spray with nonstick cooking spray.

3. Remove chicken from marinade; discard marinade. Cook in batches 15 to 20 minutes or until chicken is browned, cooked through (165°F) and no longer pink in center.

EASY TERIYAKI BURGERS

MAKES 6 SERVINGS

- 1 **pound lean ground beef**
- ½ **cup plain dry bread crumbs**
- ¼ **cup low-sodium ketchup**
- 2 **tablespoons low-sodium teriyaki sauce**
- ½ **teaspoon black pepper**
- 6 **Kaiser rolls or hamburger buns, warmed**
- 6 **leaves green leaf lettuce**
- 6 **slices tomato**

1. Combine beef, bread crumbs, ketchup, teriyaki sauce and pepper in large bowl; mix well. Shape beef into 6 (½-inch-thick) patties.

2. Preheat air fryer to 370°F.

3. Cook in batches 8 to 10 minutes, flipping halfway through cooking, until desired doneness. Place patties on rolls. Serve with lettuce and tomato slices.

BANG-BANG CHICKEN ON RICE

MAKES 4 SERVINGS

CREAMY HOT SAUCE

- ½ cup mayonnaise
- ¼ cup sweet chili sauce
- 1½ teaspoons hot pepper sauce

CHICKEN

- 1 pound chicken breasts, cut into 1-inch pieces
- ¾ cup panko bread crumbs
- ½ cup all-purpose flour
- 2 green onions, chopped
- Hot cooked rice (optional)

1. Prepare Creamy Hot Sauce. Combine mayonnaise, chili sauce and hot pepper sauce in medium bowl. Divide mixture in half; set one half aside.

2. Put chicken in large bowl. Place panko in shallow dish.

3. Using hands, toss chicken with flour until well coated. Dip chicken pieces in Creamy Hot Sauce, then coat in panko. Spray with nonstick cooking spray.

4. Preheat air fryer to 390°F. Line basket with parchment paper.

5. Cook chicken in batches 10 to 12 minutes or until golden brown. Remove chicken to large bowl; drizzle with remaining Creamy Hot Sauce.

6. Sprinkle with green onions. Serve over rice, if desired.

GREEK CHICKEN BURGERS WITH CUCUMBER YOGURT SAUCE

MAKES 4 SERVINGS

½ cup plus 2 tablespoons plain nonfat Greek yogurt

½ medium cucumber, peeled, seeded and finely chopped

Juice of ½ lemon

3 cloves garlic, minced and divided

2 teaspoons finely chopped fresh mint *or* ½ teaspoon dried mint

⅛ teaspoon salt

⅛ teaspoon ground white pepper

BURGERS

1 pound ground chicken breast

3 ounces crumbled reduced-fat feta cheese

4 large kalamata olives, rinsed, patted dry and minced

1 egg

½ to 1 teaspoon dried oregano

¼ teaspoon black pepper

Mixed baby lettuce (optional)

Fresh mint leaves (optional)

1. Combine yogurt, cucumber, lemon juice, 2 cloves garlic, 2 teaspoons chopped mint, salt and white pepper in medium bowl; mix well. Cover and refrigerate until ready to serve.

2. For burgers, combine chicken, feta cheese, olives, egg, oregano, black pepper and remaining 1 clove garlic in large bowl; mix well. Shape mixture into 4 patties.

3. Preheat air fryer to 370°F. Spray basket with nonstick cooking spray. Cook 12 to 15 minutes or until cooked through (165°F).

4. Serve burgers with sauce and mixed greens, if desired. Garnish with mint leaves.

STEAK, MUSHROOMS & ONIONS

MAKES 4 SERVINGS

¾ **pound boneless steak, cut into 1-inch cubes**

8 **ounces sliced mushrooms, cleaned and washed**

1 **small onion, chopped**

3 **tablespoons melted butter, divided**

1 **teaspoon Worcestershire sauce**

½ **teaspoon garlic powder**

½ **teaspoon salt**

¼ **teaspoon black pepper**

Hot cooked egg noodles (optional)

½ **teaspoon dried parsley flakes**

1. Combine steak pieces, mushrooms and onion in large bowl. Toss with 1½ tablespoons butter, Worcestershire sauce and garlic powder.

2. Preheat air fryer to 390°F. Line basket with foil. Cook steak mixture 10 to 12 minutes, shaking occasionally, until steak is cooked.

3. Remove steak mixture to large bowl. Toss with remaining 1½ tablespoons butter, salt and pepper.

4. Serve over noodles, if desired. Sprinkle with parsley flakes.

EASY AIR-FRIED CHICKEN THIGHS

MAKES 4 SERVINGS

8 bone-in or boneless chicken thighs with skin (about 1½ pounds)

½ teaspoon garlic powder

½ teaspoon onion powder

½ teaspoon dried oregano

½ teaspoon ground thyme

½ teaspoon paprika

¼ teaspoon salt

½ teaspoon black pepper

1. Place chicken in large resealable food storage bag. Combine garlic powder, onion powder, oregano, thyme, paprika, salt and pepper in small bowl; mix well. Add to chicken; shake until spices are distributed.

2. Preheat air fryer to 350°F. Line basket with parchment paper; spray with nonstick cooking spray.

3. Cook in batches 20 to 25 minutes or until golden brown and cooked through (165°F), turning chicken halfway through cooking.

PARMESAN-COATED CHICKEN

MAKES 4 SERVINGS

½ cup mayonnaise

4 boneless skinless chicken breasts (about 4 ounces each)

¼ cup Italian seasoned dry bread crumbs

2 tablespoons grated Parmesan cheese

1. Spread mayonnaise generously over chicken. Combine bread crumbs and Parmesan cheese in shallow dish.

2. Coat chicken with bread crumb mixture.

3. Preheat air fryer to 370°F.

4. Cook 12 to 15 minutes or until cooked through (165°F.) and golden brown.

SERVING SUGGESTION: Serve this dish with assorted vegetables like broccoli and carrots.

SPICY SALMON

MAKES 4 SERVINGS

½ **teaspoon ground cumin**
½ **teaspoon chili powder**
¼ **teaspoon salt**

¼ **teaspoon black pepper**
¼ **teaspoon paprika**
4 **salmon fillets (about 4 ounces each)**

1. Combine cumin, chili powder, salt, pepper and paprika in small bowl. Rub over top of salmon.

2. Preheat air fryer to 350°F. Line basket with parchment paper; spray with nonstick cooking spray.

3. Cook in batches 8 to 10 minutes or until salmon is lightly crispy and flakes easily when tested with a fork.

SERVING SUGGESTION: Serve with tossed salad and rice.

BAKED PANKO CHICKEN

MAKES 2 SERVINGS

½ **cup panko bread crumbs**

3 **teaspoons assorted dried herbs (such as rosemary, basil, parsley, thyme or oregano), divided**

Salt and black pepper

2 **tablespoons mayonnaise**

2 **boneless skinless chicken breasts**

1. Combine panko, 1 teaspoon herbs, salt and pepper in shallow dish. Combine mayonnaise and remaining 2 teaspoons herbs in small bowl. Spread mayonnaise mixture onto chicken. Coat chicken with panko mixture, pressing to adhere.

2. Preheat air fryer to 370°F. Line basket with parchment paper; spray with nonstick cooking spray.

3. Cook 12 to 15 minutes or until chicken is browned, cooked through (165°F) and no longer pink in center.

CHICKEN WITH HERB STUFFING

MAKES 4 SERVINGS

⅓ cup fresh basil leaves

1 package (8 ounces) goat cheese with garlic and herbs

4 boneless skinless chicken breasts

1 tablespoon olive oil

1. Place basil in food processor; process using on/off pulsing action until chopped. Cut goat cheese into large pieces and add to food processor; process using on/off pulsing action until combined.

2. Place 1 chicken breast on cutting board and cover with plastic wrap. Pound with meat mallet until ¼ inch thick. Repeat with remaining chicken.

3. Shape about 2 tablespoons of cheese mixture into log and set in center of each chicken breast. Wrap chicken around filling to enclose completely. Tie securely with kitchen string. Drizzle with oil.

4. Preheat air fryer to 370°F. Cook 15 to 20 minutes or until chicken is cooked through (165°F) and filling is hot. Allow to cool slightly, remove string and slice to serve.

SNACKS
& CHIPS

THICK POTATO CHIPS WITH BEER KETCHUP

MAKES 4 SERVINGS

Beer Ketchup (recipe follows)

2 baking potatoes, unpeeled
Sea salt and black pepper

1. Prepare Beer Ketchup; set aside.

2. Slice potatoes into ⅛- to ¼-inch-thick slices; place in large bowl. Spray with nonstick cooking spray. Sprinkle with salt and pepper.

3. Preheat air fryer to 390°F. Cook in batches 12 to 15 minutes or until crispy and golden brown, shaking occasionally and separating potatoes that stick together.

4. Serve potatoes with Beer Ketchup.

BEER KETCHUP

MAKES ABOUT 1 CUP

¾ cup ketchup

¼ cup beer

1 tablespoon Worcestershire sauce

¼ teaspoon onion powder

Ground red pepper

Mix all ingredients in small saucepan. Bring to a boil. Reduce heat; simmer 2 to 3 minutes. Remove from heat and let cool. Cover and store in refrigerator until ready to use.

BITE-YOU-BACK ROASTED EDAMAME

MAKES 4 SERVINGS

2 teaspoons vegetable oil

2 teaspoons honey

¼ teaspoon wasabi powder*

1 package (about 12 ounces) shelled edamame, thawed if frozen

Kosher salt (optional)

Wasabi powder can be found in the Asian section of most supermarkets and in Asian specialty markets.

1. Combine oil, honey and wasabi powder in large bowl; mix well. Add edamame; toss to coat.

2. Preheat air fryer to 370°F.

3. Cook 12 to 14 minutes, shaking occasionally during cooking, until lightly browned. Remove from basket to large bowl; sprinkle generously with salt, if desired. Cool completely before serving. Store in airtight container.

EASY WONTON CHIPS

MAKES 2 DOZEN CHIPS (4 SERVINGS)

1½ **teaspoons soy sauce**

1 **teaspoon peanut or vegetable oil**

½ **teaspoon sugar**

¼ **teaspoon garlic salt**

12 **wonton wrappers**

1. Combine soy sauce, oil, sugar and garlic salt in small bowl; mix well.

2. Cut wonton wrappers diagonally in half. Spray with nonstick cooking spray. Brush soy sauce mixture lightly over both sides.

3. Preheat air fryer to 370°F. Cook in batches 3 to 5 minutes, shaking halfway through cooking, until crisp and lightly browned. Transfer to wire rack; cool completely.

PARMESAN-CRUSTED FRENCH FRIES WITH ROSEMARY DIPPING SAUCE

MAKES 4 SERVINGS

3 medium baking potatoes (8 ounces each), peeled and cut into 12 wedges

1 tablespoon olive oil

⅛ teaspoon salt

⅛ teaspoon black pepper

¼ cup shredded Parmesan cheese

DIPPING SAUCE

½ cup mayonnaise

1 teaspoon chopped fresh rosemary *or* ½ teaspoon dried rosemary

½ teaspoon grated lemon peel

1 clove garlic, crushed

1. Toss potatoes with oil, salt and pepper in medium bowl.

2. Preheat air fryer to 390°F. Cook in batches 18 to 20 minutes, shaking halfway through cooking. Sprinkle Parmesan cheese over potatoes. Cook additional 3 to 5 minutes until cheese melts and potatoes are tender.

3. For dipping sauce, stir together mayonnaise, rosemary, lemon peel and garlic in small bowl. Serve potatoes with dipping sauce.

CINNAMON TOAST POPPERS

MAKES 12 SERVINGS

6 cups fresh bread* cubes (1-inch cubes)

2 tablespoons butter, melted

1½ tablespoons sugar

½ teaspoon ground cinnamon

Use a firm sourdough, whole wheat or semolina bread.

1. Place bread cubes in large bowl. Drizzle with butter; toss to coat.

2. Combine sugar and cinnamon in small bowl. Sprinkle over bread cubes; mix well.

3. Preheat air fryer to 350°F. Cook 10 to 12 minutes, shaking occasionally during cooking, until bread is golden and fragrant. Serve warm or at room temperature.

HAPPY APPLE SALSA WITH CINNAMON PITA CHIPS

MAKES 3 SERVINGS

- 2 teaspoons sugar
- ¼ teaspoon ground cinnamon
- 2 pita bread rounds, split
- 1 tablespoon jelly or jam
- 1 medium apple, diced
- 1 tablespoon finely diced celery
- 1 tablespoon finely diced carrot
- 1 tablespoon golden raisins
- 1 teaspoon lemon juice

1. Combine sugar and cinnamon in small bowl. Cut pita rounds into wedges. Spray with nonstick cooking spray; sprinkle with cinnamon-sugar.

2. Preheat air fryer to 350°F.

3. Cook 8 to 10 minutes, shaking occasionally, until lightly browned. Set aside to cool.

4. Meanwhile, place jelly in medium microwavable bowl; microwave on HIGH 10 seconds. Stir in apple, celery, carrot, raisins and lemon juice. Serve salsa with pita chips.

SPICED SESAME WONTON CRISPS

MAKES 4 SERVINGS

1 tablespoon water
2 teaspoons olive oil
½ teaspoon paprika
½ teaspoon ground cumin or chili powder

¼ teaspoon dry mustard
10 (3-inch) wonton wrappers, cut into strips
Sesame seeds

1. Combine water, oil, paprika, cumin and mustard in small bowl; mix well.

2. Lightly brush wonton strips with oil mixture. Sprinkle with sesame seeds.

3. Preheat air fryer to 350°F. Spray basket with nonstick cooking spray.

4. Cook in single layer in batches 4 to 5 minutes or until browned and crunchy, flipping halfway through cooking. Remove to plate; cool completely.

NOTE: Your wonton crisps may curl up in the air fryer while cooking. They will be just as tasty, if they do.

EGGPLANT NIBBLES

MAKES 4 SERVINGS

1 egg
1 tablespoon water
½ cup seasoned dry bread
   crumbs

1 Asian eggplant or 1 small
   globe eggplant
Marinara sauce, heated
   (optional)

1. Beat egg and water in shallow dish. Place bread crumbs in another shallow dish.

2. Cut ends off of eggplant. Cut into sticks about 3 inches long by ½-inch wide.

3. Coat eggplant sticks in egg, letting excess drip back into dish, then roll in bread crumbs. Spray with olive oil cooking spray.

4. Preheat air fryer to 370°F. Line basket with foil or parchment paper.

5. Cook in batches 12 to 14 minutes, shaking occasionally during cooking, until eggplant is tender and lightly browned. Serve with warm marinara sauce, if desired.

HERBED POTATO CHIPS

MAKES 2 SERVINGS

1 tablespoon minced fresh dill, thyme or rosemary leaves *or* 1 teaspoon dried dill weed, thyme or rosemary

¼ teaspoon garlic salt

⅛ teaspoon black pepper

2 medium red potatoes

¾ cup sour cream (optional)

1. Combine dill, garlic salt and pepper in small bowl; set aside.

2. Cut potatoes crosswise into very thin slices, about $\frac{1}{16}$ inch thick. Pat dry with paper towels. Spray potatoes with nonstick cooking spray; sprinkle evenly with seasoning mixture.

3. Preheat air fryer to 390°F. Line basket with parchment paper; spray with cooking spray.

4. Cook 10 to 12 minutes, shaking during cooking and spraying occasionally with cooking spray until golden brown.

5. Cool. Serve with sour cream, if desired.

KALE CHIPS

MAKES 6 SERVINGS

1 **large bunch kale (about 1 pound)**

1 **tablespoon olive oil**

1 **teaspoon garlic powder**

½ **teaspoon salt**

½ **teaspoon black pepper**

---

1. Wash kale and pat dry with paper towels. Remove center ribs and stems; discard. Cut leaves into 2- to 3-inch-wide pieces.

2. Combine kale leaves, oil, garlic powder, salt and pepper in large bowl; toss to coat.

3. Preheat air fryer to 390°F.

4. Cook in batches 3 to 4 minutes or until edges are lightly browned and leaves are crisp. Cool completely. Store in airtight container.

SAVORY PITA CHIPS

MAKES 4 SERVINGS

2 whole wheat or white pita
bread rounds
2 tablespoons grated
Parmesan cheese

1 teaspoon dried basil
¼ teaspoon garlic powder

1. Carefully cut each pita round in half horizontally; split into 2 rounds. Cut each round into 6 wedges. Spray wedges with nonstick cooking spray.

2. Combine Parmesan cheese, basil and garlic powder in small bowl; sprinkle evenly over pita wedges.

3. Preheat air fryer to 350°F.

4. Cook 8 to 10 minutes, shaking occasionally during cooking, until golden brown. Cool completely.

CINNAMON CRISPS: Substitute butter-flavored cooking spray for nonstick cooking spray and 1 tablespoon sugar mixed with ¼ teaspoon ground cinnamon for Parmesan cheese, basil and garlic powder.

CINNAMON-SUGAR TWISTS

MAKES 14 TWISTS

1 package (8 ounces) refrigerated crescent roll dough

½ cup coarse sugar

1 teaspoon ground cinnamon

1. Unroll dough on work surface. Cut crosswise into 1-inch strips. Roll strips to form thin ropes; fold in half and twist halves together. Combine sugar and cinnamon in shallow dish.

2. Preheat air fryer to 370°F. Line basket with parchment paper; spray with nonstick cooking spray.

3. Cook in batches 6 to 8 minutes or until golden brown. Spray with cooking spray; roll in cinnamon-sugar mixture to coat. Serve warm.

CORN TORTILLA CHIPS

MAKES 3 DOZEN CHIPS (ABOUT 12 SERVINGS)

6 **(6-inch) corn tortillas, preferably day-old**

½ **teaspoon salt**

Salsa or guacamole (optional)

---

1. If tortillas are fresh, let stand, uncovered, in single layer on wire rack 1 to 2 hours to dry slightly.

2. Stack tortillas; cut tortillas into 6 equal wedges. Spray tortillas generously with nonstick olive oil cooking spray.

3. Preheat air fryer to 370°F.

4. Cook in batches 5 to 6 minutes, shaking halfway through cooking. Sprinkle with salt. Serve with salsa or guacamole, if desired.

NOTE: Tortilla chips are served with salsa as a snack, used as the base for nachos and used as scoops for guacamole, other dips or refried beans. They are best eaten fresh, but can be stored, tightly covered, in a cool place 2 or 3 days.

ROASTED CHICKPEAS

MAKES 1 CUP

1 can (about 15 ounces) chickpeas, rinsed and drained

1 tablespoon olive oil

¼ teaspoon salt

¼ teaspoon black pepper

¼ tablespoon chili powder

¼ teaspoon ground red pepper

1 lime, cut into wedges

1. Combine chickpeas, oil, salt and black pepper in large bowl. Toss to mix well.

2. Preheat air fryer to 390°F.

3. Cook 8 to 10 minutes, shaking occasionally during cooking, until chickpeas begin to brown.

4. Sprinkle with chili powder and ground red pepper. Serve with lime wedges, if desired.

NOTE: Great as a snack or as a topping for salads. Chickpeas offer a delicious crunch and healthier alternative to croutons.

SPLENDID SIDES

CURLY AIR-FRIED FRIES

MAKES 4 SERVINGS

2 **large russet potatoes, unpeeled**
¼ **cup finely chopped onion**
1 **teaspoon vegetable oil**

½ **teaspoon salt**
¼ **teaspoon black pepper**
Honey mustard dipping sauce, ketchup or other favorite dipping sauce

---

1. Spiral potatoes with thick spiral blade of spiralizer.*

2. Place potatoes and onion in large bowl; drizzle with oil. Toss well.

3. Preheat air fryer to 390°F. Line basket with parchment paper. Cook 10 to 12 minutes or until golden brown and crispy, shaking occasionally during cooking. Sprinkle with salt and pepper.

4. Serve with dipping sauce.

If you do not have a spiralizer, cut potatoes into thin strips.

FRIED GREEN TOMATOES

MAKES 4 SERVINGS

⅓ cup all-purpose flour

¼ teaspoon salt

2 eggs

1 tablespoon water

½ cup panko bread crumbs

2 large green tomatoes, cut into ½-inch-thick slices

½ cup ranch dressing

1 tablespoon sriracha sauce

1 package (5 ounces) spring greens salad mix

¼ cup crumbled goat cheese

1. Combine flour and salt in shallow dish. Beat eggs and water in another shallow dish. Place panko in third shallow dish. Coat tomato slices with flour, shaking off excess. Dip in egg mixture, letting excess drip back into bowl. Roll in panko to coat. Place on plate.

2. Preheat air fryer to 370°F. Line basket with parchment paper.

3. Cook in batches 6 to 8 minutes or until golden brown.

4. Combine ranch dressing and sriracha in small bowl; mix well. Divide greens among 4 serving plates; top with tomatoes. Drizzle with dressing mixture; sprinkle with cheese.

SWEET POTATO FRIES

MAKES 2 SERVINGS

2 **sweet potatoes, peeled and sliced**

1 **tablespoon olive oil**

¼ **teaspoon coarse salt**

¼ **teaspoon black pepper**

1. Toss potatoes with oil, salt and pepper in medium bowl.

2. Preheat air fryer to 390°F. Spray basket with nonstick cooking spray.

3. Cook 10 to 12 minutes, shaking occasionally during cooking, until lightly browned.

GARLIC KNOTS

MAKES 20 KNOTS

4 **tablespoons (½ stick) butter, divided**

1 **tablespoon olive oil**

1 **tablespoon minced garlic**

½ **teaspoon salt**

¼ **teaspoon garlic powder**

1 **package (about 11 ounces) refrigerated bread dough**

½ **cup grated Parmesan cheese**

2 **tablespoons chopped fresh parsley**

½ **teaspoon dried oregano**

1. Melt 2 tablespoons butter in small saucepan over low heat. Add oil, garlic, salt and garlic powder; cook over very low heat 5 minutes. Pour into small bowl; set aside.

2. Roll out dough into 8×10-inch rectangle. Cut into 20 squares. Roll each piece into 8-inch rope; tie in a knot. Brush knots with garlic mixture.

3. Preheat air fryer to 370°F. Line basket with parchment paper.

4. Cook in batches 8 to 10 minutes or until knots are lightly browned. Meanwhile, melt remaining 2 tablespoons butter. Combine Parmesan cheese, parsley and oregano in small bowl; mix well. Brush melted butter over warm knots; immediately sprinkle with cheese mixture. Cool slightly; serve warm.

CRISPY FRIES WITH HERBED DIPPING SAUCE

MAKES 3 SERVINGS

Herbed Dipping Sauce
(recipe follows)
2 large unpeeled baking
potatoes

1 tablespoon vegetable oil
½ teaspoon kosher salt

1. Prepare Herbed Dipping Sauce; set aside.

2. Cut potatoes into ¼-inch strips. Toss potato strips with oil in large bowl to coat evenly.

3. Preheat air fryer to 390°F. Spray basket with nonstick cooking spray.

4. Cook in batches 12 to 15 minutes, shaking occasionally during cooking, until golden brown and crispy. Sprinkle with salt. Serve immediately with Herbed Dipping Sauce.

HERBED DIPPING SAUCE: Stir ¼ cup mayonnaise, 1 tablespoon chopped fresh herbs (such as basil, parsley, oregano and/or dill), ¼ teaspoon salt and ⅛ teaspoon black pepper in small bowl until smooth and well blended. Cover and refrigerate until ready to serve.

ZUCCHINI FRITTE

MAKES 4 SERVINGS

Lemon Aioli (recipe follows)

¾ to 1 cup soda water

½ cup all-purpose flour

¼ cup cornstarch

½ teaspoon coarse salt, plus additional for serving

¼ teaspoon garlic powder

¼ teaspoon dried oregano

¼ teaspoon black pepper

3 cups panko bread crumbs

1½ pounds medium zucchini (about 8 inches long), ends trimmed, cut lengthwise into ¼-inch-thick slices

¼ cup grated Parmesan or Romano cheese

Chopped fresh parsley

Lemon wedges

1. Prepare Lemon Aioli; cover and refrigerate until ready to use.

2. Pour ¾ cup soda water into large bowl. Combine flour, cornstarch, ½ teaspoon salt, garlic powder, oregano and pepper in medium bowl; mix well. Gradually whisk flour mixture into soda water just until blended. Add additional soda water, if necessary, to reach consistency of thin pancake batter. Place panko in shallow dish.

3. Working with one at a time, dip zucchini slices into batter to coat; let excess batter drip back into bowl. Add to panko; pressing into zucchini slices to coat both sides completely.

4. Preheat air fryer to 390°F. Line basket with parchment paper.

5. Cook in batches 7 to 10 minutes or until golden brown. Sprinkle with Parmesan cheese and parsley. Serve with Lemon Aioli and lemon wedges.

LEMON AIOLI: Combine ½ cup mayonnaise, 2 tablespoons lemon juice, 1 tablespoon chopped fresh Italian parsley and 1 clove minced garlic in small bowl; mix well. Season with salt and pepper.

AIR-FRIED CAULIFLOWER FLORETS

MAKES 4 SERVINGS

1 head cauliflower

1 tablespoon olive oil

3 tablespoons grated Parmesan cheese

2 tablespoons panko bread crumbs

½ teaspoon salt

½ teaspoon chopped fresh parsley

¼ teaspoon ground black pepper

1. Cut cauliflower into florets. Place in large bowl. Drizzle with oil. Sprinkle Parmesan cheese, panko, salt, parsley and pepper over cauliflower; toss to coat.

2. Preheat air fryer to 390°F. Spray basket with nonstick cooking spray.

3. Cook in batches 12 to 15 minutes or until browned, shaking every 5 minutes during cooking.

ORANGE GLAZED CARROTS

MAKES 6 SERVINGS

1 package (32 ounces) baby carrots

1 tablespoon packed light brown sugar

1 tablespoon orange juice

1 tablespoon melted butter

¼ teaspoon ground cinnamon

⅛ teaspoon ground nutmeg

Orange peel and fresh chopped parsley (optional)

1. Place carrots in large bowl. Combine brown sugar, orange juice and butter in small bowl. Pour over carrots; toss well.

2. Preheat air fryer to 390°F.

3. Cook 6 to 8 minutes, shaking occasionally during cooking, until carrots are tender and lightly browned. Remove to serving dish. Sprinkle with cinnamon and nutmeg. Garnish with orange peel and parsley.

GARLIC AIR-FRIED FRIES

MAKES 4 SERVINGS

2 large potatoes, peeled and cut into matchstick strips

2 teaspoons plus 1 tablespoon olive oil, divided

1½ teaspoons minced garlic

½ teaspoon dried parsley flakes

½ teaspoon salt

¼ teaspoon ground black pepper

Ketchup, blue cheese or ranch dressing (optional)

1. Combine potato strips and 2 teaspoons oil in medium bowl; toss well.

2. Preheat air fryer to 390°F. Line basket with parchment paper.

3. Cook in batches 8 to 10 minutes, tossing occasionally, until golden brown and crispy.

4. While fries are cooking, combine remaining 1 tablespoon oil, garlic, parsley flakes, salt and pepper in small bowl.

5. Toss warm fries with garlic sauce. Serve immediately with ketchup, blue cheese or ranch dressing, if desired.

POTATO BALLS

MAKES 20 BALLS

2 cups refrigerated leftover mashed potatoes*

2 tablespoons all-purpose flour, plus additional for rolling balls

⅔ cup shredded reduced-fat Cheddar cheese

¼ cup chopped green onions

1 large egg

½ teaspoon salt

¼ teaspoon black pepper

1½ cups seasoned dry bread crumbs

If you don't have leftover potatoes, prepare 2 cups instant mashed potatoes and refrigerate at least 1 hour.

1. Combine potatoes, 2 tablespoons flour, cheese and green onions in large bowl. Scoop out about 2 tablespoons mixture and roll into a 1-inch ball, adding additional flour, if necessary, making about 20 balls.

2. Beat egg, salt and pepper in medium bowl. Place bread crumbs in shallow dish. Dip balls in egg, letting excess drip back into bowl, then roll in bread crumbs until fully coated. Place on baking sheet; refrigerate 30 minutes.

3. Preheat air fryer to 390°F. Spray basket with nonstick cooking spray.

4. Cook in batches 8 to 10 minutes or until balls are browned and heated through.

CHEESY GARLIC BREAD

MAKES 4 TO 6 SERVINGS

1 loaf (about 8 ounces)
Italian bread

¼ cup (½ stick) butter,
softened

4 cloves garlic, diced

2 tablespoons grated
Parmesan cheese

1 cup (4 ounces) shredded
mozzarella cheese

---

1. Cut bread in half horizontally. Spread cut sides of bread evenly with butter; top with garlic. Sprinkle with Parmesan and mozzarella cheeses.

2. Preheat air fryer to 370°F. Line basket with foil.

3. Cook 5 to 6 minutes or until cheese is melted and golden brown. Cut crosswise into slices. Serve warm.

PARMESAN POTATO WEDGES

MAKES 6 SERVINGS

2 pounds unpeeled red potatoes

2 tablespoons butter, melted

1½ teaspoons dried oregano

½ teaspoon salt

Black pepper

2 tablespoons grated Parmesan cheese

1. Boil potatoes in salted water 8 to 10 minutes or until fork-tender. Drain. Cool completely.

2. Cut cooled potatoes into wedges; place in large bowl. Add butter, oregano, salt and pepper; mix gently.

3. Preheat air fryer to 390°F. Line basket with parchment paper.

4. Cook potatoes 10 to 12 minutes, shaking occasionally during cooking, until golden brown and crispy. Place in large bowl; toss with Parmesan cheese.

AIR-FRIED CORN-ON-THE-COB

MAKES 2 SERVINGS

2 teaspoons butter, melted

¼ teaspoon salt

½ teaspoon black pepper

½ teaspoon chopped fresh parsley

2 ears corn, husks and silks removed

Foil

Grated Parmesan cheese (optional)

1. Combine butter, salt, pepper and parsley in small bowl. Brush corn with butter mixture. Wrap each ear of corn in foil.*

2. Preheat air fryer to 390°F. Cook 10 to 12 minutes, turning halfway through cooking. Sprinkle with Parmesan cheese before serving, if desired.

If your air fryer basket is on the smaller side, you may need to break ears of corn in half to fit.

BUTTERNUT SQUASH FRIES

MAKES 4 SERVINGS

½ teaspoon garlic powder

¼ teaspoon salt

¼ teaspoon ground red pepper

1 butternut squash (about 2½ pounds), peeled, seeded and cut into 2-inch-thin slices

2 teaspoons vegetable oil

1. Combine garlic powder, salt and ground red pepper in small bowl; set aside.

2. Place squash in large bowl. Drizzle with oil and sprinkle with seasoning mix; gently toss to coat.

3. Preheat air fryer to 390°F. Cook in batches 16 to 18 minutes, shaking halfway during cooking, until squash is tender and begins to brown.

ZUCCHINI TOMATO ROUNDS

MAKES 4 SERVINGS

- 2 **large zucchini**
- **Foil**
- ½ **cup cherry tomatoes, sliced**
- 1 **tablespoon olive oil**

- 2 **cloves garlic, minced**
- 2 **teaspoons Italian seasoning**
- 1 **teaspoon grated Parmesan cheese**

1. Cut zucchini into thin slices three-fourths of the way down (do not cut all the way through). Place zucchini on foil sprayed with nonstick cooking spray.

2. Place tomato slices between each zucchini slice. Combine oil and garlic in small bowl. Drizzle over zucchini. Sprinkle with Italian seasoning and Parmesan cheese. Wrap foil around zucchini.

3. Preheat air fryer to 390°F. Place foil packets in basket. Cook 10 to 12 minutes or until browned and softened.

AIR-FRIED FRIES

MAKES 2 SERVINGS

2 **small russet potatoes
(10 ounces),
refrigerated**

2 **teaspoons olive oil**
¼ **teaspoon salt or onion salt**

1. Peel potatoes and cut lengthwise into ¼-inch strips. Place in colander; rinse under cold running water 2 minutes. Drain. Pat dry with paper towels.

2. Place potatoes in large resealable food storage bag. Drizzle with oil. Seal bag; shake to coat evenly.

3. Preheat air fryer to 390°F. Cook 15 to 18 minutes, shaking occasionally during cooking, until light brown and crisp. Sprinkle with salt.

NOTE: Refrigerating potatoes—usually not recommended for storage—converts the starch in the potatoes to sugar, which enhances the browning when the potatoes are baked. Do not refrigerate the potatoes longer than 2 days, because they may develop a sweet flavor.

FRIED GREEN TOMATO PARMESAN

MAKES 2 SERVINGS

1 can (15 ounces) no-salt-added tomato sauce, divided

2 green tomatoes

Salt and black pepper

¼ cup all-purpose flour

½ teaspoon Italian seasoning

1 egg

1 tablespoon water

¾ cup panko bread crumbs

¼ cup shredded Parmesan cheese

Shredded fresh basil

Hot cooked spaghetti (optional)

1. Spread ½ cup tomato sauce in small baking dish that fits inside air fryer basket.

2. Cut tomatoes into ¼-inch slices. Lightly season with salt and pepper, if desired.

3. Combine flour and Italian seasoning in shallow dish. Whisk egg and water in another shallow dish. Place panko in third shallow dish. Coat tomatoes with flour mixture. Dip in egg mixture. Dredge in panko, pressing onto all sides.

4. Preheat air fryer to 350°F. Cook tomatoes in batches 2 to 3 minutes per side or until panko is golden brown. Remove tomatoes to sauce in baking dish, slightly overlapping. Sprinkle with Parmesan cheese and ½ cup tomato sauce.

5. Cook 6 to 8 minutes or until cheese is melted and sauce is heated through. Sprinkle with basil. Serve with spaghetti, if desired, and remaining tomato sauce.

PESTO-PARMESAN TWISTS

MAKES 24 BREADSTICKS

1 package (about 11 ounces) refrigerated bread dough

¼ cup prepared pesto

⅔ cup grated Parmesan cheese, divided

1 tablespoon olive oil

1. Roll out dough into 20×10-inch rectangle on lightly floured surface. Spread pesto evenly over half of dough; sprinkle with ⅓ cup Parmesan cheese. Fold remaining half of dough over filling, forming 10-inch square.

2. Cut into 12 (1-inch) strips with sharp knife. Cut strips in half crosswise to form 24 strips total. Twist each strip several times.

3. Brush breadsticks with oil; sprinkle with remaining ⅓ cup Parmesan cheese.

4. Preheat air fryer to 370°F. Cook in batches 8 to 10 minutes or until golden brown. Serve warm.

GREEN BEAN FRIES

MAKES 6 SERVINGS

DIPPING SAUCE

- ½ **cup light mayonnaise**
- ¼ **cup light sour cream**
- ¼ **cup low-fat buttermilk**
- ¼ **cup minced peeled cucumber**
- 1½ **teaspoons lemon juice**
- 1 **clove garlic**
- 1 **teaspoon wasabi powder**
- 1 **teaspoon prepared horseradish**
- ½ **teaspoon dried dill weed**
- ½ **teaspoon dried parsley flakes**
- ½ **teaspoon salt**
- ⅛ **teaspoon ground red pepper**

GREEN BEAN FRIES

- 8 **ounces fresh green beans, trimmed**
- ⅓ **cup all-purpose flour**
- ⅓ **cup cornstarch**
- ½ **cup reduced-fat (2%) milk**
- 1 **egg**
- ¾ **cup plain dry bread crumbs**
- 1 **teaspoon salt**
- ½ **teaspoon onion powder**
- ¼ **teaspoon garlic powder**

1. For dipping sauce, combine mayonnaise, sour cream, buttermilk, cucumber, lemon juice, garlic, wasabi powder, horseradish, dill weed, parsley flakes, salt and ground red pepper in blender; blend until smooth. Refrigerate until ready to use.

2. For green bean fries, bring large saucepan of salted water to a boil. Add green beans; cook 4 minutes or until crisp-tender. Drain and run under cold running water to stop cooking.

3. Combine flour and cornstarch in large bowl. Whisk milk and egg in another large bowl. Combine bread crumbs, salt, onion powder and garlic powder in shallow dish. Place green beans in flour mixture; toss to coat. Working in batches, coat beans with egg mixture, letting excess drain back into bowl. Roll green beans in bread crumb mixture to coat.

4. Preheat air fryer to 390°F. Cook in batches 6 to 8 minutes, shaking occasionally during cooking, until golden brown. Serve warm with dipping sauce.

IRRESISTIBLE TREATS

CHOCOLATE CHERRY TURNOVERS

MAKES 4 TURNOVERS

1 package (8 ounces) refrigerated crescent roll dough

¾ cup semisweet chocolate chips, divided

½ cup canned cherry pie filling

1. Unroll dough onto clean work surface; separate into 4 rectangles. Press perforations firmly to seal. Cut off corners of rectangles with sharp paring knife to form oval shapes.

2. Place 1 tablespoon chocolate chips on half of each oval; top with 2 tablespoons pie filling. Sprinkle with additional 1 tablespoon chocolate chips. Fold dough over filling; press edges to seal. Crimp edges with fork, if desired.

3. Preheat air fryer to 370°F. Spray basket with nonstick cooking spray.

4. Cook in batches 8 to 10 minutes or until golden brown. Cool on wire rack 5 minutes. Melt remaining chocolate chips and drizzle over turnovers. Serve warm.

DOUGHNUT HOLE FONDUE

MAKES 5 SERVINGS

- 1 **package (about 6 ounces) refrigerated biscuit dough (5 biscuits)**
- 3 **tablespoons butter, divided**
- 1 **tablespoon sugar**
- ¼ **teaspoon ground cinnamon**
- ¾ **cup whipping cream**
- 1 **cup bittersweet or semisweet chocolate chips**
- ½ **teaspoon vanilla**
- **Sliced fresh fruit, such as pineapple, strawberries and cantaloupe**

1. Separate biscuits into 5 portions. Cut each in half; roll dough into balls to create 10 balls.

2. Place 2 tablespoons butter in small microwavable bowl. Microwave on HIGH 30 seconds or until melted; stir. Combine sugar and cinnamon in small dish. Dip balls in melted butter; roll in cinnamon-sugar mixture.

3. Preheat air fryer to 370°F. Spray basket with nonstick cooking spray.

4. Cook in batches 4 to 5 minutes or until golden brown.

5. Meanwhile, heat cream in small saucepan until bubbles form around edge. Remove from heat. Add chocolate; let stand 2 minutes or until softened. Add remaining 1 tablespoon butter and vanilla; whisk until smooth. Keep warm in fondue pot or transfer to serving bowl.

6. Serve with doughnut holes and fruit.

FRUIT TARTS

MAKES 2 SERVINGS

1 refrigerated pie crust (half of a 15-ounce package)

1 tablespoon melted butter

¼ cup apple, cherry or blueberry pie filling

Coarse sugar

1. Unroll pie crust on clean work surface; cut into 4 pieces. Brush butter over dough. Spread pie filling over 2 pieces of dough; top each with second piece of dough. Seal edges by crimping with tines of a fork. Brush tops with butter; sprinkle with sugar.

2. Preheat air fryer to 370°F. Line basket with parchment paper.

3. Cook 6 to 8 minutes or until light golden brown. Remove to plate; cool.

MAPLE WALNUT APPLE CRESCENT COBBLER

MAKES 8 SERVINGS

FILLING

- **6 Golden Delicious apples (2½ pounds), peeled and thinly sliced**
- **⅓ cup maple syrup**
- **2 tablespoons all-purpose flour**
- **2 teaspoons vanilla**
- **⅛ teaspoon ground nutmeg**

TOPPING

- **1 package (8 ounces) refrigerated crescent roll dough**
- **4 teaspoons butter, melted**
- **¼ cup chopped walnuts**
- **2 tablespoons packed brown sugar**

1. Spray 8 ramekins* with nonstick cooking spray. Combine apples, maple syrup, flour, vanilla and nutmeg in medium bowl; toss to coat. Spoon into prepared ramekins.

2. Preheat air fryer to 370°F. Cook 12 to 14 minutes or until apples are tender but still firm.

3. Meanwhile, divide crescent roll dough into 8 triangles; place on work surface. Brush top of each triangle with butter. Combine walnuts and brown sugar in small bowl; sprinkle over dough. Roll up each dough triangle to form crescent. Arrange crescents over warm apple mixture.

4. Cook 5 to 7 minutes or until filling is thick and bubbly and crescent rolls are golden brown.

If you do not have 8 ramekins, prepare 4 at a time.

TOASTED POUND CAKE WITH BERRIES AND CREAM

MAKES 4 SERVINGS

1 **frozen pound cake, thawed**

2 **tablespoons melted butter**

1 **cup fresh blackberries or blueberries**

1 **cup fresh raspberries or strawberries**

Whipped topping, vanilla ice cream or prepared lemon curd

---

1. Cut pound cake into 8 slices. Brush both sides of cake with butter.

2. Preheat air fryer to 370°F. Cook in batches 5 to 7 minutes, turning halfway through cooking, until cake is lightly browned.

3. Serve with fresh berries, whipped topping, ice cream or lemon curd, as desired.

FRIED PINEAPPLE WITH TOASTED COCONUT

MAKES 8 SERVINGS

1 large pineapple, cored and cut into chunks

½ cup packed brown sugar

1 teaspoon ground cinnamon

½ teaspoon ground nutmeg

½ cup toasted coconut*

Ice cream or whipped cream (optional)

Chopped macadamia nuts (optional)

Maraschino cherries (optional)

To toast coconut in air fryer, place coconut in small ramekin. Cook in preheated air fryer at 350°F 2 to 3 minutes or until lightly browned.

1. Place pineapple chunks in large bowl. Combine brown sugar, cinnamon and nutmeg in small bowl; sprinkle over pineapple. Toss well. Refrigerate 30 minutes.

2. Preheat air fryer to 370°F. Spray basket with nonstick cooking spray.

3. Cook 6 to 8 minutes or until pineapple is browned and lightly crispy. Sprinkle with coconut. Serve with ice cream and/or macadamia nuts, if desired. Garnish with maraschino cherry.

CANDY CALZONE

MAKES 16 SERVINGS

1 package small chocolate, peanut and nougat candy bars, chocolate peanut butter cups or other chocolate candy bar (8 bars)

1 package (about 15 ounces) refrigerated pie crusts (2 crusts)

½ cup milk chocolate chips

1. Chop candy into ¼-inch pieces.

2. Unroll pie crusts on cutting board or clean surface. Cut out 3-inch circles with biscuit cutter. Place about 1 tablespoon chopped candy on one side of each circle; fold dough over candy to form semicircle. Crimp edges with fingers or fork to seal.

3. Preheat air fryer to 370°F. Line basket with parchment paper. Cook in batches 8 to 10 minutes or until golden brown. Remove to wire rack to cool slightly.

4. Place chocolate chips in small microwavable bowl; microwave on HIGH 1 minute. Stir; microwave in 30-second intervals, stirring until smooth. Drizzle melted chocolate over calzones; serve warm.

HASSELBACK APPLES

MAKES 4 SERVINGS

2 **medium apples, unpeeled**
   Foil

2 **tablespoons packed
   brown sugar**

2 **tablespoons finely
   chopped walnuts**

½ **teaspoon ground
   cinnamon**

2 **tablespoons butter,
   melted**

½ **cup vanilla ice cream
   (optional)**

1. Cut apples in half vertically. Scoop out seeds. Lay flat side down; cut slits ⅛ inch apart almost all the way down. Place apples on foil; wrapping lightly up sides of apple.

2. Combine brown sugar, walnuts and cinnamon in small bowl. Brush butter over tops of apples, letting drip inside slits. Sprinkle apples with brown sugar mixture.

3. Preheat air fryer to 350°F. Place foil-wrapped apples in basket. Cook 12 to 15 minutes or until apples are softened and browned.

4. Serve with ice cream, if desired.

NOTE: If apples brown too quickly on top, brush with additional melted butter.

AIR-FRIED S'MORES

MAKES 2 SERVINGS

2   whole graham crackers,
      broken in half

     Foil

2   marshmallows

1   package (1.5 ounces) milk
      chocolate candy bar,
      broken in half

1. Place 2 graham cracker squares on 2 sheets of foil. Top each with marshmallows. Gather foil around graham crackers.

2. Preheat air fryer to 370°F. Cook 1½ to 2 minutes or until marshmallows are browned.

3. Remove carefully from basket. Top marshmallows with chocolate bar halves and remaining graham cracker squares. Bring sides together to create sandwich.

PLUM-GINGER BRUSCHETTA

MAKES 9 SERVINGS

- 1 sheet frozen puff pastry (half of 17¼-ounce package), thawed
- 2 cups chopped unpeeled firm ripe plums (about 3 medium)
- 2 tablespoons sugar
- 2 tablespoons chopped candied ginger
- 1 tablespoon all-purpose flour
- 2 teaspoons lemon juice
- ⅛ teaspoon ground cinnamon
- 2 tablespoons apple jelly *or* apricot preserves

1. Cut puff pastry sheet lengthwise into 3 strips. Cut each strip crosswise in thirds to make 9 pieces.

2. Preheat air fryer to 370°F. Line basket with parchment paper. Cook in batches 5 to 6 minutes or until puffed and lightly browned.

3. Meanwhile, combine plums, sugar, ginger, flour, lemon juice and cinnamon in medium bowl.

4. Gently brush each puff pastry piece with about ½ teaspoon jelly; top with scant ¼ cup plum mixture. Cook in batches 1 to 2 minutes or until fruit is tender.

CHOCOLATE ROLLS

MAKES 16 ROLLS

8 tablespoons granulated sugar, divided

1 package (about 15 ounces) refrigerated pie crusts (2 crusts)

1 cup semisweet chocolate chips

1 egg white

Powdered sugar (optional)

1. Sprinkle 2 tablespoons granulated sugar on cutting board or work surface. Roll out one pie crust over sugar. Sprinkle pie crust with 2 tablespoons granulated sugar. Using pizza wheel or sharp knife, trim away 1 inch dough from 4 sides to form square. (Save dough trimmings for another use or discard.)

2. Cut square in half; cut each half crosswise into 4 pieces to form 8 small (4×2-inch) rectangles. Place heaping teaspoon chocolate chips at one short end of each rectangle; roll up, enclosing chocolate chips. Brush lightly with egg white. Repeat with remaining crust.

3. Preheat air fryer to 370°F. Spray basket with nonstick cooking spray.

4. Cook in batches 8 to 10 minutes or until lightly browned. Cool 10 minutes to serve warm, or cool completely. Sprinkle with powdered sugar, if desired.

APPLE PIE POCKETS

MAKES 4 SERVINGS

- 2 pieces lavash bread, each cut into 4 rectangles
- 2 tablespoons melted butter
- ¾ cup apple pie filling
- 1 egg, lightly beaten with 1 teaspoon water
- ½ cup powdered sugar
- ⅛ teaspoon ground cinnamon
- 2½ teaspoons milk

1. Brush 1 side of each piece of lavash with butter. Place half of the pieces, buttered-side down, on work surface. Spoon 3 tablespoons pie filling in center of each lavash, leaving ½-inch border uncovered. Using pastry brush, brush border with egg wash. Top with remaining lavash pieces, buttered-side up. Using tines of fork, press edges together to seal. Use paring knife to cut 3 small slits in center of each pie pocket.

2. Preheat air fryer to 370°F. Line basket with parchment paper.

3. Cook in batches 8 to 10 minutes or until crust is golden and crisp. Remove to wire rack; cool 15 minutes.

4. Combine powdered sugar, cinnamon and milk in small bowl; whisk until smooth. Drizzle over pockets; let stand 15 minutes to allow glaze to slightly set.

SUGAR-AND-SPICE TWISTS

MAKES 12 SERVINGS

2 tablespoons granulated sugar

½ teaspoon ground cinnamon

1 package (about 11 ounces) refrigerated breadstick dough (12 breadsticks)

---

1. Combine sugar and cinnamon in shallow dish or plate. Separate breadsticks; roll each piece into 12-inch rope. Roll ropes in sugar-cinnamon mixture to coat. Twist each rope into pretzel shape.

2. Preheat air fryer to 370°F. Line basket with parchment paper; spray with nonstick cooking spray.

3. Cook in batches 8 to 10 minutes or until lightly browned. Remove to wire rack to cool 5 minutes. Serve warm.

HINT: Use colored sugar sprinkles in place of the granulated sugar in this recipe for a fun "twist" of color perfect for holidays, birthdays or simple everyday celebrations.

POUND CAKE DIP STICKS

MAKES 8 TO 10 SERVINGS

½ cup raspberry jam, divided

1 package (10¾ ounces) frozen pound cake

1½ cups cold whipping cream

1. Microwave ¼ cup jam on HIGH 30 seconds or until smooth. Cut pound cake into 10 (½-inch) slices. Brush 1 side of slices lightly with warm jam. Cut each slice lengthwise into 3 sticks.

2. Preheat air fryer to 390°F. Spray basket with nonstick cooking spray.

3. Cook in batches 5 to 6 minutes or until cake sticks are crisp and light golden brown. Remove to wire rack.

4. Meanwhile, beat whipping cream in large bowl with electric mixer until soft peaks form. Add remaining ¼ cup raspberry jam; beat until combined. Serve pound cake dip sticks with raspberry whipped cream.

CHOCOLATE FRUIT TARTS
MAKES 6 TARTS

1 refrigerated pie crust (half of 15-ounce package)

1¼ cups prepared low-fat chocolate pudding (about 4 snack-size pudding cups)

Fresh sliced strawberries, raspberries, blackberries or favorite fruit

---

1. Spray 6 (2½-inch) silicone muffin cups with nonstick cooking spray. Unfold pie crust on lightly-floured surface. Let stand at room temperature 15 minutes.

2. Roll out pie crust on clean work surface; cut out 6 circles with 4-inch round cookie cutter. Place dough circles in muffin cups, pleating around sides of cups. (Press firmly to hold dough in place.) Prick bottom and sides with fork.

3. Preheat air fryer to 370°F. Cook in batches 8 to 10 minutes or until golden brown. Carefully remove tart shells from muffin cups. Cool completely on wire rack.

4. Fill each tart shell with about 3 tablespoons pudding; arrange fruit on top.

INDEX

INDEX

INDEX

METRIC CONVERSION CHART

VOLUME MEASUREMENTS (dry)

1/8 teaspoon = 0.5 mL
1/4 teaspoon = 1 mL
1/2 teaspoon = 2 mL
3/4 teaspoon = 4 mL
1 teaspoon = 5 mL
1 tablespoon = 15 mL
2 tablespoons = 30 mL
1/4 cup = 60 mL
1/3 cup = 75 mL
1/2 cup = 125 mL
2/3 cup = 150 mL
3/4 cup = 175 mL
1 cup = 250 mL
2 cups = 1 pint = 500 mL
3 cups = 750 mL
4 cups = 1 quart = 1 L

VOLUME MEASUREMENTS (fluid)

1 fluid ounce (2 tablespoons) = 30 mL
4 fluid ounces (1/2 cup) = 125 mL
8 fluid ounces (1 cup) = 250 mL
12 fluid ounces (1 1/2 cups) = 375 mL
16 fluid ounces (2 cups) = 500 mL

WEIGHTS (mass)

1/2 ounce = 15 g
1 ounce = 30 g
3 ounces = 90 g
4 ounces = 120 g
8 ounces = 225 g
10 ounces = 285 g
12 ounces = 360 g
16 ounces = 1 pound = 450 g

DIMENSIONS

1/16 inch = 2 mm
1/8 inch = 3 mm
1/4 inch = 6 mm
1/2 inch = 1.5 cm
3/4 inch = 2 cm
1 inch = 2.5 cm

OVEN TEMPERATURES

250°F = 120°C
275°F = 140°C
300°F = 150°C
325°F = 160°C
350°F = 180°C
375°F = 190°C
400°F = 200°C
425°F = 220°C
450°F = 230°C

BAKING PAN SIZES

Utensil	Size in Inches/Quarts	Metric Volume	Size in Centimeters
Baking or	8×8×2	2 L	20×20×5
Cake Pan	9×9×2	2.5 L	23×23×5
(square or	12×8×2	3 L	30×20×5
rectangular)	13×9×2	3.5 L	33×23×5
Loaf Pan	8×4×3	1.5 L	20×10×7
	9×5×3	2 L	23×13×7
Round Layer	8×1½	1.2 L	20×4
Cake Pan	9×1½	1.5 L	23×4
Pie Plate	8×1¼	750 mL	20×3
	9×1¼	1 L	23×3
Baking Dish	1 quart	1 L	—
or Casserole	1½ quart	1.5 L	—
	2 quart	2 L	—